Adobe® Photoshop® 5.5

SAMS

A Division of Macmillan USA
201 W. 103rd Street
Indianapolis, Indiana 46290

Daniel Giordan

Visually in Full Color

How To Use Adobe Photoshop 5.5

International Standard Book Number: 0-672-31719-2

Library of Congress Catalog Card Number: 99-65587

Printed in the United States of America

First Printing: December 1999

01   00   99   4   3   2   1

Trademarks

All terms mentioned in this book that are known to be trademarks or service marks have been appropriately capitalized. Sams cannot attest to the accuracy of this information. Use of a term in this book should not be regarded as affecting the validity of any trademark or service mark.

Warning and Disclaimer

Every effort has been made to make this book as complete and as accurate as possible, but no warranty or fitness is implied. The information provided is on an "as is" basis. The author and the publisher shall have neither liability nor responsibility to any person or entity with respect to any loss or damages arising from the information contained in this book.

Acquisitions Editor
Randi Roger

Development Editor
Alice Martina Smith

Managing Editor
Charlotte Clapp

Project Editor
Carol Bowers

Copy Editor
Fran Blauw

Indexer
Heather McNeill

Proofreader
Mary Ellen Stephenson

Technical Assistant
T. Michael Clark

Technical Editor
Robert Stanley

Interior Designer
Nathan Clement

Cover Designers
Nathan Clement
Aren Howell

Contents at a Glance

Contents

About the Author

Daniel Giordan is an artist and designer who works as the director of Creative Services for the eCommerce Corporation. In addition to this book, he has authored three other books on Photoshop, including *Using Photoshop* and *Dynamic Photoshop*. He has written other books that address subjects such as Dreamweaver, Kai's PowerTools, and general design subjects. Dan writes a monthly column, "Giordan on Photoshop," for *Digital Camera* magazine and is the creator of "Giordan on Graphics," a biweekly Internet column on graphic design that is part of the WebReference.com Web site (www.webreference.com).

With a master's degree in fine arts, Dan also paints and works with photography while indulging an excessive interest in capturing every waking moment of his son's life on film.

Dedication

This book is for Barb and Josh.

Acknowledgements

Where do I start here? So many thanks, so little time....

Let me start by thanking everyone at Adobe for building the software application most responsible for the ongoing evolution and refinement in computer graphics. Photoshop is the world's most popular design program, and it is supporting ongoing advancements into digital photography, Web design, and many other creative developments. Nothing else even comes close.

Let me also acknowledge **Randi Roger**, acquisitions editor at Macmillan Computer Publishing. I've known Randi for years, and although I've helped her out in the past on a few projects, this was our first solo book together. You're a real pro, Randi...the best I've ever worked with. Thanks for all your support. Let's not wait two more years to do another project.

I also want to thank **Alice Martina Smith**, **Robert Stanley**, and the whole team of editors and designers at Macmillan USA and Sams Publishing.

When I start feeling like my part of the project is overwhelming, I think about these people who are juggling details and deadlines for up to 12 different titles at a time. And all I have to worry about is what's on page 56.

Thanks also goes to **T. Michael Clark** for assistance in finishing this book in a timely manner.

Finally, I must thank God and my family for all their support. Writing a book is a huge task that consumes the overwhelming majority of your time and attention. Even when you're not writing, you're thinking about content, solutions, and upcoming deadlines. Although I've made every effort to keep **Barb** and **Josh** in my sights, I'm sure that my attention has slipped over the past few weeks. Thank you, Barb, for putting up with the schedule, my moods, and my absence. I thank God every day for you and Josh, and I thank Him for what He's done for all of us.

Tell Us What You Think!

As the reader of this book, *you* are our most important critic and commentator. We value your opinion and want to know what we're doing right, what we could do better, what areas you'd like to see us publish in, and any other words of wisdom you're willing to pass our way.

You can fax, email, or write me directly to let me know what you did or didn't like about this book—as well as what we can do to make our books stronger.

Please note that I cannot help you with technical problems related to the topic of this book, and that because of the high volume of mail I receive, I might not be able to reply to every message.

When you write, please be sure to include this book's title and author, as well as your name and phone or fax number. I will carefully review your comments and share them with the author and editors who worked on the book.

Fax: 317-581-4770

Email: graphics_sams@mcp.com

Mail: Mark Taber
       Associate Publisher
       Sams Publishing
       201 West 103rd Street
       Indianapolis, IN 46290 USA

How to Use This Book

The Complete Visual Reference

Each part of this book consists of a series of short instructional tasks designed to help you understand all the information you need to get the most out of Photoshop.

Click: Click the left mouse button once.

Double-click: Click the left mouse button twice in rapid succession.

Right-click: Click the right mouse button once.

Selection: Highlights the area onscreen discussed in the step or task.

Keyboard: Type information or data into the indicated location.

Click & Drag

Release

Drag & drop: Position the mouse pointer over the object, click and hold the left mouse button, drag the object to its new location, and release the mouse button.

Key icons: Clearly indicate which key combinations to use.

Each task includes a series of easy-to-understand steps designed to guide you through the procedure.

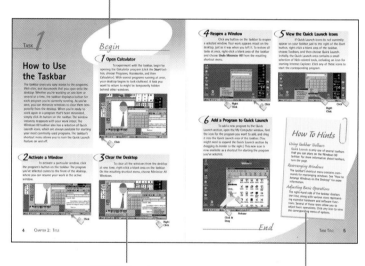

Each step is fully illustrated to show you how it looks onscreen.

Extra hints that tell you how to accomplish a goal are provided in most tasks.

Screen elements (such as menus, icons, windows, and so on), as well as things you enter or select, appear in **boldface** type.

Continues

If you see this symbol, it means the task you're in continues on the next page.

Introduction

$\mathcal{T}$he history of image-editing applications should be divided into two categories: BP and AP (Before Photoshop and After Photoshop). Before Photoshop, there were various bitmap applications available, some of which were very good. There was Pixel Paint Pro, Studio 8, Digital Darkroom, and, of course, MacPaint. Like dinosaurs facing extinction, all these applications faded away after the comet called Photoshop fell to earth in the late 1980s.

I am told that Photoshop got its start as a file-conversion program at Industrial Light and Magic, the special-effects studio started by George Lucas. This was the mid-'80s, when graphics file formats were all over the map and PostScript was non-existent. Photoshop began as an application that converted one format to another. One look at the extensive list of Photoshop's **Save As** file options, and this begins to make some sense.

One could argue that Photoshop is the most influential facilitator for the growth of digital graphics since the Macintosh. And although the Mac got us started in the mid-'80s, Adobe has kept things moving forward with interface standards and cross-platform compatibility that make graphics accessible to just about every computer in the world. This universality has made Photoshop the core application driving new advances in the computer graphics world. Photoshop combines with After Effects for professional video editing, with Quark and InDesign for industry-standard page layout, and with Illustrator and FreeHand for desktop illustration. In all these instances, Photoshop sits right in the middle. Photoshop also drives the advancement of digital photography and professional Web design.

It was the boom in Web design books in the early '90s that prompted Adobe to launch a complementary application to Photoshop called ImageReady. Although Photoshop was the creative powerhouse, ImageReady excelled in prepping images for the Web; compressing file sizes; converting colors; and building clean, concise animations. ImageReady also featured a bare-bones set of image-editing tools for basic image editing.

From the day it was first released, many people asked why ImageReady wasn't built in to Photoshop as a plug-in. So many of the editing features were redundant, and its main attractions were conversion tools, compression, and GIF animation. With the release of Photoshop 5.5 in July 1999, it appears that Adobe finally got the message. The company announced that it is bundling ImageReady as a free application included with Photoshop 5.5. To make things even easier, Adobe built in a **Jump To** button that jumps back and forth between the two applications effortlessly, preserving history states, layers, and every other file component.

Because this book covers Photoshop 5.5, it also addresses how ImageReady supports graphic design workflow and integration with Photoshop, especially where Web design is concerned. Therefore, you will see ImageReady written into some of the task instructions—and even featured in a few standalone tasks. Because of the redundant feature set created when they were separate programs, many of the tasks described for Photoshop can be executed in virtually the same way in ImageReady.

And another thing—because Adobe does such an excellent job of building cross-platform applications, you should not be concerned that all the screen shots in the book are Mac-based. Everything works the same in Windows (except for the keystrokes, which I've identified for both systems).

Whether you're working with ImageReady or Photoshop, this book is designed to get you up and running quickly, with straightforward solutions to your questions. The challenge comes from the fact that Photoshop's complexity cannot be clearly addressed in seven steps or less. I've tried to address the details as much as I can, expounding in the How-To Hints sections and task and part openers. Although the format of this book resists long narratives and detailed explanations, a ton of solid information is still packed into the tasks that follow. I was very pleased that we were able to drill a bit deeper into some of the advanced features in this book, and I hope it helps you push things further and get the most out of Photoshop.

Task

Getting Started with Photoshop

Most people look at Photoshop as a program with many levels of complexity. They say things like "I probably don't use 10 percent of the program," or "I just use it to open my digital camera images." Although it's true that Photoshop has a deep level of complexity, it's also true that the program is easy for the beginner to use. This is one of the features that has made Photoshop so popular: It's easy to jump in and get started, and as your needs grow, the program grows right along with you.

The first step in getting started is to set up Photoshop to work the way you want it to work. How do you set the preferences? What about customizing the desktop or setting ruler increments? You should consider a few customizable features, as well as specific tools built into the program that can come in handy with just about any file you might be working on.

Because Adobe is shipping ImageReady 2.0 along with Photoshop 5.5, you also should consider how to optimize ImageReady for the way you work, as well as how ImageReady integrates with Photoshop. ●

Welcome to Photoshop and ImageReady

This task is a basic introduction to Photoshop and ImageReady. In this task, you launch each program and evaluate the general workspace.

Begin

1 Launch Photoshop

To launch Photoshop in Windows, click the **Start** button and choose **Programs, Adobe, Photoshop 5.5, Adobe Photoshop 5.5**. To launch Photoshop on a Mac, open the folder labeled **Adobe Photoshop 5.5** and double-click the **Adobe Photoshop 5.5** icon.

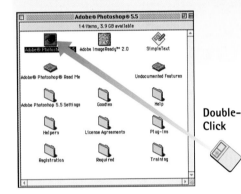

Double-Click

2 Close the Wizards

The first time you launch Photoshop, you see the **Adobe Color Management Assistant**. This short assistant helps you calibrate your monitor and set the RGB color-handling options for Photoshop. If you have time, go through the steps: Click the **Open Adobe Gamma Wizard** button at the bottom of the first screen. The Gamma Wizard helps you calibrate your monitor and then walks you through the setup of RGB features. If you don't want to run the wizard at this time, click the **Cancel** button. You can run the wizard from Photoshop at any time by choosing **Help, Color Management**.

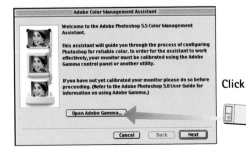

Click

3 The Basic Photoshop Screen Areas

After closing the wizard, you'll see the full range of Photoshop controls arranged on your screen. The **toolbox** is in the upper-left corner and contains all the Photoshop tool options. All the Photoshop **palettes** appear on the right side, and the **menu bar** appears across the top of the screen.

Toolbox   Menu bar   Palettes

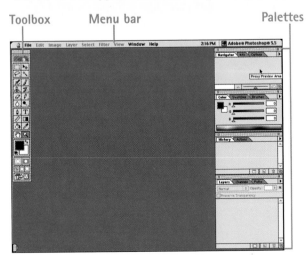

4 Launch ImageReady

To launch ImageReady in Windows, click the **Start** button and choose **Programs, Adobe, Photoshop 5.5, Adobe ImageReady 2.0**. To launch ImageReady on a Mac, open the folder labeled **Adobe Photoshop 5.5** and double-click the **Adobe ImageReady 2.0** icon.

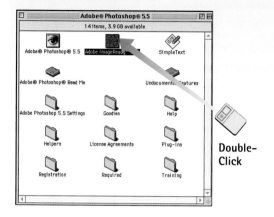

Double-Click

5 The Basic ImageReady Screen Areas

You will find that the ImageReady desktop looks very similar to the Photoshop desktop. Closer examination reveals that some of the tool icons and palettes are different and that an **Animation** palette appears in the lower-left corner of the screen.

Toolbox   Menu bar   Animation pallete   Palettes

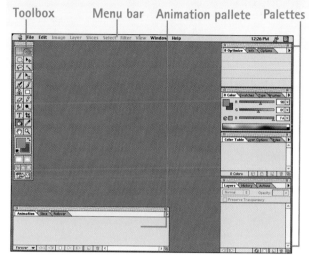

End

How-To Hints

Photoshop or ImageReady?

Because the desktops for Photoshop and ImageReady look so similar, you sometimes may wonder which application you're in. A quick way to verify your location is to look at the top of the tool-box. In Photoshop, the toolbox has a cropped eye; in ImageReady, the toolbox has a multicolored compass.

Jump from Photoshop to ImageReady

Switching from Photoshop to ImageReady is as easy as clicking the **Jump To** button at the bottom of the toolbox. (This button is sometimes called the **Launch** button.)If you are in Photoshop when you click this button, ImageReady opens (if you haven't already launched ImageReady, clicking the **Jump To** button does that for you). If you're in ImageReady when you click **Jump To**, Photoshop opens (and launches, if necessary).

How to Use the Toolbox

Each time you launch Photoshop, the toolbox appears on the screen, usually in the upper-left corner. In the process of editing an image, you will go to the toolbox frequently to choose various selection, painting, and specialty tools. This task outlines what you'll find in the toolbox and how to access it.

Begin

1 Open the Photoshop Toolbox

The toolbox should appear automatically on the desktop, but it can be closed, which means you'll have to reopen it. To open the toolbox, choose **Window, Show Tools**.

2 Select a Photoshop Tool

Click a tool to select it. If the tool button contains a small triangle in the lower-right corner, that tool offers additional tool options in a pop-out menu. Click and hold the tool button to view the pop-out menu; drag through the pop-out menu to select one of the additional tools.

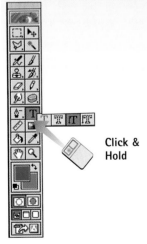

Click & Hold

3 Open the ImageReady Toolbox

The ImageReady toolbox should appear on the desktop as soon as ImageReady opens. Like its Photoshop counterpart, the ImageReady toolbox also can be closed, requiring you to reopen it. To open the toolbox in ImageReady, choose **Window, Show Tools**.

4 Select an ImageReady Tool

Click a tool to select it. If the tool button contains a small triangle in the lower-right corner, that tool offers additional tool options in a pop-out menu. Click and hold the tool button to view the pop-out menu; drag through the pop-out menu to select one of the additional tools.

Click & Hold

5 Jump Between Applications

Click the **Jump To** button at the bottom of either the Photoshop or the ImageReady toolbox to move between Photoshop and ImageReady. This technique is especially useful when you have a file open and want to use features from both applications.

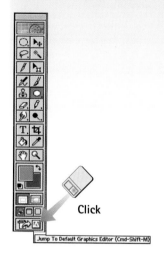

Click

Jump To Default Graphics Editor (Cmd-Shift-M)

End

How-To Hints

Path to Adobe Online

Click the **Adobe Online** button at the top of the toolbox (the eye icon in Photoshop or the compass icon in ImageReady) to access the **Adobe.com** Web site.

Configure the Jump To button

By default, you can jump to Photoshop or ImageReady by clicking the **Jump To** button. You can access alternative graphics and HTML editors as well by creating a shortcut or alias to a desired application and dragging it to the following location: **Adobe Photoshop 5.5, Helpers, Jump to Graphics Editor**.

TASK

How to Use the Menu Bars

The menu bars in Photoshop and ImageReady operate like the menu bars in any other application. Click the menu name so that the menu drops down. Choose an option that has a solid right-facing arrowhead, and a submenu pops out. Choose an option that has a three-dot ellipsis...) following it, and a dialog box opens. Click *any* option to choose it. This task looks at the grouping of the different menus to help you understand the functionality associated with each menu.

1 Photoshop File Menu

You use the Photoshop **File** menu to address the basic opening, closing, and saving of files. This menu covers the import/export of files, automated tasks, preferences, and color settings for the overall application as well. It also contains the **Quit** command (**Exit** in Windows) for closing down the application.

2 Photoshop Edit and Image Menus

You use the Photoshop **Edit** and **Image** menus to specify most of the standard global changes to an open image. You'll find controls for cut and paste, as well as transformations, fill, stroke, and pattern on the **Edit** menu. On the **Image** menu, you'll find options for color mode, canvas and image size, and global color adjustments.

3 Photoshop Layer Menu

The Photoshop **Layer** menu covers all your layer options—creating and deleting layers, merging, applying layer effects, and grouping. You can find most of these same controls on the **Layers** *palette menu*.

4 Photoshop Select Menu

You use the Photoshop **Select** menu to control selection options within the program. These options include inverting selections, feathering, selection modifiers, and saving and loading selections.

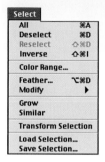

5 Photoshop Filter Menu

Simply put, the Photoshop **Filter** menu contains all 101 of the native Photoshop filters, divided into 14 subheadings. The **Filter** menu also can include any third-party filters you may have loaded in the Photoshop plug-ins folder.

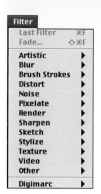

6 Photoshop View and Window Menus

You use the **View** menu to control zooming and previews, as well as the visibility of rulers and guides. The **Window** menu lets you launch and close any of the 12 palettes. In addition, the **Window** menu lists all open file windows, so that you can move a file to the front of the screen simply by choosing it from this menu.

7 Help Menus

The ImageReady and Photoshop **Help** menus enable you to turn balloon help on and off (for the Macintosh), as well as to access help by topic. The Windows version of the **Help** menu offers two **About** options, which provide version information about Photoshop and plug-ins. In addition, the Photoshop **Help** menu gives you access to all the color wizards.

Photoshop Help Menu   ImageReady Help Menu

Continues

8 ImageReady File Menu

You use the ImageReady **File** menu to open, close, and save files, as well as to save files optimized as GIFs or JPEGs. This menu also covers the import and export of files, HTML browser previews, preferences, and recent files. The **File** menu also contains the **Quit** command (**Exit** in Windows) for closing down the application.

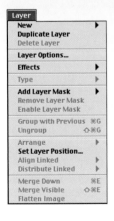

9 ImageReady Edit and Image Menus

You use the ImageReady **Edit** and **Image** menus to control most of the standard global changes to an open image. Controls for cutting and pasting image data and HTML, as well as options for transformations, fill, stroke, and pattern are located on the **Edit** menu. The **Image** menu is more limited than its Photoshop counterpart; it offers canvas and image size controls, as well as a few global color adjustments.

10 ImageReady Layer Menu

The ImageReady **Layer** menu covers all your layer options—creating and deleting layers, merging, applying layer effects, and grouping. It also offers control over layer-to-imagemap conversion (from the **Layer Options** selection), and precise layer placement. You can find many of these same controls in the **Layers** palette menu.

11 ImageReady Slices Menu

You use the **Slices** menu to specify how image slices are created, modified, linked, and deleted. If it has to do with slices, you'll find that option on this menu.

12 ImageReady Select Menu

You use the ImageReady **Select** menu to control selection options within the program. These options include inverting selections, feathering, selection modifiers, and saving and loading selections.

13 ImageReady Filter Menu

The ImageReady **Filter** menu contains 80 ImageReady filters, divided into 13 subheadings. This menu also includes any third-party filters you may have loaded into the plug-ins folder.

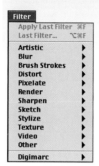

14 ImageReady View and Window Menus

You use the **View** menu to control zooming and previews, as well as the visibility of rulers and guides. The **Window** menu lets you launch and close any of the 17 ImageReady palettes. In addition, it also lists all open file windows and all the window-arrangement commands.

How-To Hints

Why Menus Are Grayed Out

Menu commands are *context sensitive*, meaning that they are accessible only if they can actually be used. For this reason, if a command is grayed out and unresponsive, that means you cannot use it in the given situation.

End

How to Use Photoshop and ImageReady Palettes

Photoshop and ImageReady use a floating palette system to group items and controls such as brushes and tool options. ImageReady uses 17 palettes; Photoshop uses 12. You can open and close palettes on demand and easily compress or expand them to optimize your workspace.

Begin

1 Examine a Group of Palettes

To open a palette in ImageReady or Photoshop, click the **Window** menu; while still holding the mouse button, choose the **Show** command related to the desired palette. To optimize your workspace, the application groups multiple palettes in a single window and separates them with tabs. If the palette you want is hidden, click its tab to bring it to the front of the window.

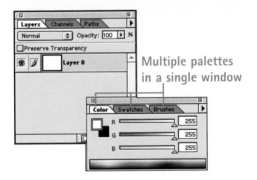

Multiple palettes in a single window

2 Collapse and Expand a Palette

To collapse or expand a palette, click the **Minimize/Maximize** button (in Windows) or the **Resize** button (on a Mac).

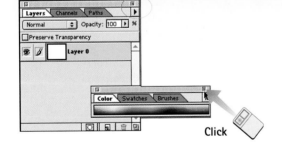

Click

3 Resize a Palette

To resize a palette, click and drag the lower-left corner of the window. To return a palette to its default size, click the **Minimize/Maximize** button (in Windows) or the **Resize** button (on a Mac).

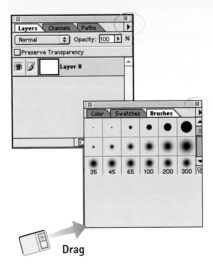

Drag

4 Tools and the Options Palette

The **Options** palette in ImageReady and Photoshop is unique in that its content varies depending on the tool selected in the toolbox. To open the **Options** palette, choose **Window, Show Options**. Alternatively, double-click a tool in the toolbox to open the **Options** palette with the parameters for that tool.

5 The Palette Menu

A **palette menu** lists options related to the functionality of the associated palette. To open any palette menu, click the black triangle in the upper-right corner of the palette and click to make a selection from the list of options.

6 Use the Palette Shortcut Buttons

At the bottom of some palettes are shortcut buttons for easy access to common tasks. To find out what each button does, first make sure that the **Show ToolTips** option is selected in the **General Preferences** dialog box (choose **File, Preferences, General**) and then position your mouse pointer over the button to read the description.

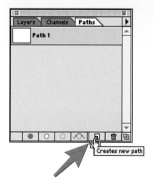

How-To Hints

Grouping Palettes

To move a palette into another palette group, click and hold the palette's tab and drag it to the target palette window. To separate a palette as a standalone window, click the tab and drag it to an empty area on the desktop. The palette will appear by itself where you release the mouse button.

Palette Placement

As you open and reposition palettes, Photoshop remembers their size and where you used them last; when you open Photoshop again, the program reopens the palettes in the same spots and at the same window sizes. To reset the palettes to their defaults each time you open them, choose **File, Preferences, General**; the **General Preferences** dialog box opens. Disable the **Save Palette Locations** option. You must restart Photoshop before the changes take effect.

End

How to Use the Photoshop Color Picker

The Photoshop **Color Picker** is the standard Photoshop interface for selecting a color. It allows fast and intuitive color selection from millions of colors. The **Color Picker** also offers Pantone color matching and Web-safe color choices.

Begin

1 Set Color Picker Preferences

Choose **File, Preferences, General** to open the Preferences dialog box to the **General** page. Select **Photoshop** from the **Color Picker** drop-down list. Although you could select the Windows or Mac/Apple color picker, the Photoshop version is the recommended choice. Click **OK** to close the dialog box.

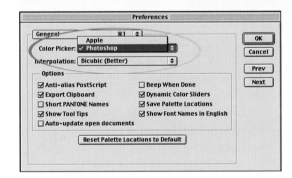

2 Launch the Color Picker

In the toolbox, click the **Foreground** color swatch to launch the **Color Picker** dialog box.

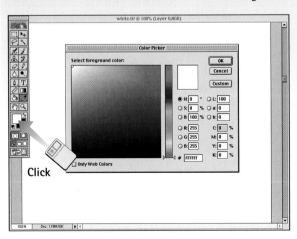

Click

3 Set the Hue

Click and drag the white triangles on the **Hue** slider to select the desired hue. As you drag, notice that the range of colors displayed in the large **Select foreground color** window changes.

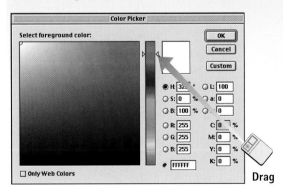

Drag

4 Select a Value

Move the cursor into the **Select foreground color** window. Notice that the cursor changes into a sample dot as you do so. Click in the color window to select a color; that color selection is reflected in the color swatch at the top right of the dialog box.

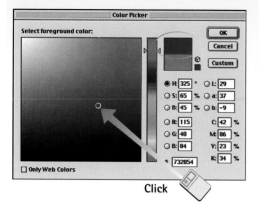

Click

5 Check the Gamut Warnings

If the color you selected falls outside the printable CMYK color gamut, a triangle with an exclamation point appears next to the selected color. The small color box that appears below the triangle indicates which color will print based on the current conversion settings. If the color you selected does not fall within the browser-safe color palette, a cube appears just below the triangle, along with another small color box that indicates the corresponding Web-safe color.

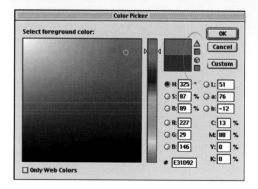

6 Select Pantone-Type Colors

In the **Color Picker**, click the **Custom** button to open the **Custom Colors** dialog box. Select a color-matching system from the **Book** drop-down list and type the color number (if you know it) or click in the color spectrum slider to select a color. Click the **Picker** button to go back to the Photoshop **Color Picker**, or click **OK** to select the color and close the color-selection dialog boxes.

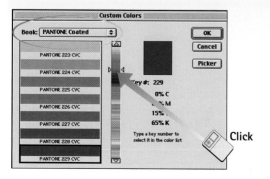

Click

How-To Hints

Comparing Relative Values

By default, the **Select foreground color** window in the **Color Picker** is based on a color's hue. Click in any of the other boxes (which represent Brightness, Saturation, RGB, or Lab) to change the way color is displayed in the window. You also can enter a numerical value in any of these fields to change the current color value numerically.

Enter a Hexadecimal Color or Check Only Web Colors

To select Web colors (colors that will display in most Web browsers), type a hexadecimal value in the # box at the bottom of the **Color Picker**. You also can enable the **Only Web Colors** check box, which changes the **Select foreground color** window so that it displays only a Web-safe color range.

End

How to Select a Color

Task 5 explained how to use the **Color Picker**. This task looks at the different ways you can specify a color in Photoshop. The methods described in this task use a combination of working with the **Color Picker**, sampling colors from images, and using preset swatches. Use the method that best suits the task at hand.

Begin

1 Select a Foreground Color

Click the **Foreground** color swatch in the toolbox to launch the **Color Picker**. Follow the steps in Task 5, "How to Use the Photoshop Color Picker," to select a color.

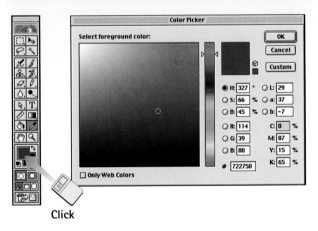

Click

2 Select a Background Color

Click the **Background** color swatch in the toolbox to launch the **Color Picker**. Follow the steps in Task 5 to select a color.

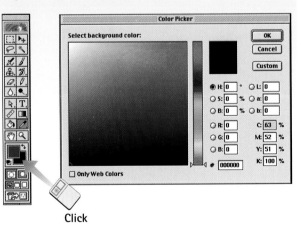

Click

3 Sample a Color

Click the **Eyedropper** tool in the toolbox. Move the tool over the color in the image you want to sample and click to select the desired color. The color you select becomes the foreground color (check the color swatch in the toolbox).

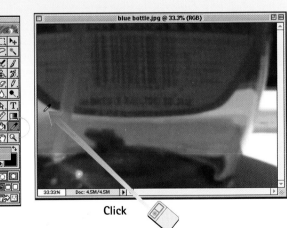

Click

4 Use the Color Palette

Choose **Window, Show Color** to open the **Color** palette. Move the RGB sliders as necessary to "mix" the desired color; watch the color you are creating in the swatch on the left side of the palette or in the toolbox. You also can select additional color models and options from the palette menu.

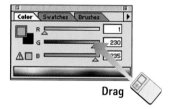

Drag

5 Use the Color Swatches

Choose **Window, Show Swatches** to open the **Swatches** palette, which contains an array of preset color swatches. Click the desired color to select it (it becomes the foreground color in the toolbox). To add the current foreground color as a swatch on this palette, move the pointer to an empty space on the palette until the pointer changes to the Paint Bucket; click to add the color as a swatch on the palette.

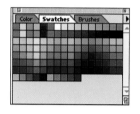

End

How-To Hints

Color Switcher

To switch the foreground and background colors, click the **Switch Colors** button (the double-headed, curved arrow to the right of the **Foreground** color swatch in the toolbox). Alternatively, press the **X** key to switch the foreground and background colors.

Revert to Black and White

Click the **Default Colors** button in the toolbox (the black square on top of the white square to the left of the **Background** color swatch) to reset the foreground and background colors to black and white. Alternatively, press the **D** key to set the foreground and background colors to black and white.

How to Use Rulers, Grids, and Guides

The importance of rulers and guides has grown considerably in the last few revisions of Photoshop. *Guides* are user-defined alignment lines. The *grid* is an underlying matrix of lines you can use for general alignment of all items on the page. The enhanced type features have made text-alignment issues much easier to address. In addition, designers are creating complete Web pages in Photoshop and ImageReady, which necessitates using guides and grids to maintain spacing and alignment.

Begin

1 Set Rulers Preferences

Choose **File, Preferences, Units & Rulers** to open the **Preferences** dialog box to the **Units and Rulers** page. From the **Units** drop-down list, choose the desired unit of measurement and click **OK**. In this instance, you do not have to restart Photoshop for the preference change to take effect.

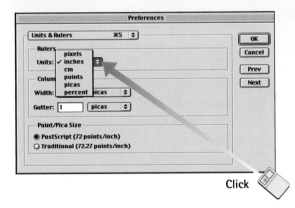

Click

2 Activate Rulers

Choose **View, Show Rulers** to make the rulers visible around the top and left edges of the image area.

Click

3 Set Guides Preferences

Choose **File, Preferences, Guides & Grid** to open the **Preferences** dialog box to the **Guides & Grid** page. Here you can specify the color and format of the guide and gridlines, as well as the spacing for the grid. Click the color swatches to select a custom color, or use the **Color** drop-down lists to select from preset colors.

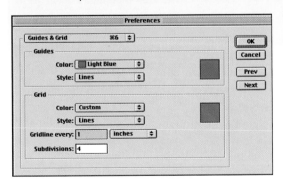

4 Create and Activate Guides

To create a guide, click the **Move** tool in the toolbox. Click in the ruler area and drag into the image area. A vertical or horizontal guide will follow the tool, depending on which ruler you started with. You can drag out as many guides as you need.

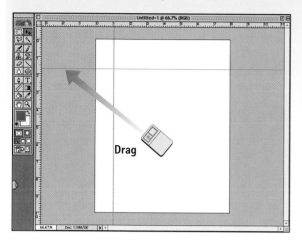

Drag

5 Set Snap-To Parameters

To precisely align elements to guides and grids as you drag the elements, choose **View, Snap to Guides** or **View, Snap to Grid**. Choose these commands again to turn them off.

6 Lock Guides as Needed

To lock the guides in place, choose **View, Lock Guides**. When you lock the guide lines, you prevent them from moving accidentally, especially when you are using numerous guides.

Click

How-To Hints

Web Measurements

When working with a Web design, set the ruler increments to pixels on the **Units & Rulers** page of the **Preferences** dialog box. Then scroll the image against the rulers to take rough measurements of page elements. An alternative way to make quick measurements is to use the **Measure** tool to measure areas within your images.

Use Guides for Precise Text Alignment

When positioning multiple text elements or multiple lines of type, use the guides feature to ensure precise alignment.

End

How to Set Up Your Workspace

When looking at images and evaluating color and sharpness, you should consider a wide range of factors. A quality monitor and high resolution certainly are important, but they can be negated by setting your monitor next to a bright window, or by frequently changing the Brightness/Contrast settings. These factors, which lie outside the system, have as much an impact on how images are viewed as anything discussed in other tasks in this part of the book.

Begin

1 Consider Monitor Placement

Try to set up your monitor to control glare from windows. Point it away from windows toward the center of the room, if possible. Consider using window shades, if necessary, to cut down on direct window lighting.

2 Control Ambient Light

As much as possible, avoid interior lights such as bright fluorescent lighting and direct desk lamps. If necessary, get a monitor shield to protect the screen from these and other ambient light sources.

3 Create an ICC Profile

Use the **Adobe Gamma Wizard** to create an ICC profile for your monitor. To do this, choose **Help, Color Management** and follow the directions in the wizard: First click the **Open Adobe Gamma** button to create your profile. Remember to save the ICC profile when you are finished with the wizard.

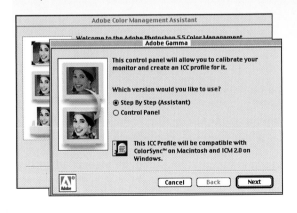

4 Set RGB as the Default Color Space

Photoshop provides numerous options for working with RGB files created on other systems. Although the actual RGB data does not change, the way it looks can change from system to system. This variation can make further editing a challenge, because you can't rely on the information your monitor displays. Run the **Adobe Color Management Assistant** to determine the best way to handle RGB images. Choose **Help, Color Management** to open the **Adobe Color Management Assistant**. Then follow the directions to pick the RGB conversion that's best for you.

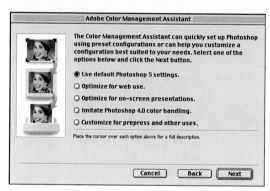

5 Create a Color Proof

After you've done all the calibration with the color wizards, it's a good idea to run a test print on a color printer and then compare the results with your monitor. Use whatever printer you use the most, even if that means sending your test print out to a service. For a subject, open and print the **CMYK Colors** image (located in the **Calibration** folder in the **Goodies** folder). Print it out and compare it with your monitor to understand how images translate to different printers.

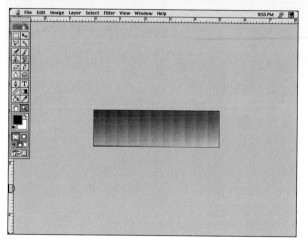

End

How-To Hints

View Your Work on More Than One Monitor

For Web work, view your work on different monitors and various platforms. Just because your system is calibrated does not mean everyone else's is. Take the time to preview and adjust your work as necessary.

Remember that you only have to create an ICC profile once (assuming that none of your system components change). Monitor phosphors do fade and change color over time, however, so you may want to recalibrate every six months or so.

Using the RGB Conversion

After you use the **Adobe Color Management Assistant** to select the conversion process you want, Photoshop handles all file conversions seamlessly for you.

How to Customize the Photoshop Desktop

Photoshop gives you lots of controls, presented in the form of tools, palettes, and menus. It also gives you control over the controls themselves, enabling you to group and arrange palettes, screen views, and other options exactly as you want to see them. You can set things up based on the way you like to work. Grouping similar palettes together and tweaking the workspace can help you work more efficiently and can help you make more logical sense out of the various tools and palettes.

Begin

1 Arrange Control Windows

Photoshop offers a default method of displaying control palettes, as indicated in the **Window** menu. The division lines in the menu indicate these groupings, which you also can see by opening any of the palettes in the menu. To customize the arrangement of the palettes, click the tab of the palette you want to move and drag it to another palette to add it to that group. Drag the palette to a blank area of the desktop to let it stand on its own.

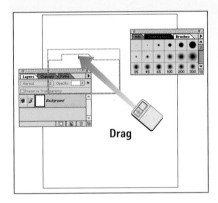
Drag

2 Set the Color Mode

If your image is not in RGB mode already, you probably should convert it to RGB before you start to work on it. RGB is one of the largest color spaces to work in and is the native color space for Web images. If your target format is different (such as CMYK or Index color), you still should convert to the larger RGB space. You then can change to another format after you finish editing the image (see Part 4, Task 1, "How to Save Files in Other Formats"). To convert to RGB, choose **Image, Mode, RGB Color**.

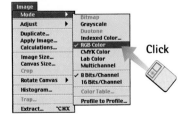
Click

3 Set Color Slider Models

Photoshop's **Color** palette (choose **Window, Show Color** to open it) features sliders that enable you to mix colors in many ways. Even if you're working on an RGB image, you still can mix colors in CMYK or HSB. To change the slider options, select any of the first six options from the **Color** palette menu.

Click

4 Create Color Swatches

Photoshop also features a color **Swatches** palette (choose **Window, Show Swatches** to open it) that lets you save a set of colors you can activate as you need it. You should build a set of swatches if you plan to reference a color repeatedly as you're working on an image. To add a swatch, set the foreground color as desired, click the **Eyedropper** tool, and then click an empty space on the **Swatches** palette. The cursor changes to the **Paint Bucket** icon as you do this. To delete a swatch, press and hold the ⌘ key (Mac users) or **Ctrl** key (Windows users), place the cursor over the desired swatch, and click. The cursor changes to a pair of scissors as you do this.

5 Select the Screen Mode

Sometimes the desktop windows in the background can be very distracting when you need to examine an image closely. You can hide the background, with or without the menus, by selecting one of the three screen display options below the foreground and background swatches colors in the toolbox.

Standard screen mode
Full-screen mode
Full-screen mode (with menu bar)

6 Use Adobe Online

If your machine is hooked up to a modem, you can access Adobe Online for tips and troubleshooting information by clicking the picture of the eye at the top of the toolbox or by choosing **File, Adobe Online**. Adobe maintains a huge library of troubleshooting suggestions and how-to tips you can access whenever you have a question.

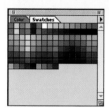

Click

How-To Hints

Keep Palette Positions from Session to Session

Select the **Save Palette Locations** option on the **General** page of the **Preferences** dialog box to keep the palette settings and positions each time you launch Photoshop.

Toggle the Display of Palettes

To quickly hide all the palettes that are currently open on the desktop, as well as the toolbox, press the **Tab** key. To redisplay all these elements, press **Tab** again.

End

How to Set Photoshop Preferences

General Controls

Choose **File, Preferences, General** to open the **Preferences** dialog box to the **General** page. You use this dialog box to control interpolation, the **Color Picker** option, and a number of other general application parameters.

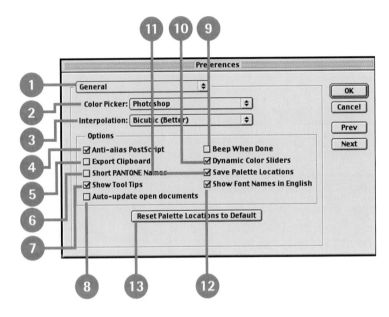

1 **Preferences Title pop-up menu:** Click the arrow to display a list of other pages in the **Preferences** dialog box; select an option to open that page.

2 **Color Picker pop-up menu:** Click the arrow to display a list of Color Picker options; select the Photoshop or Apple/Windows color picker.

3 **Interpolation pop-up menu:** Click the arrow to display a list of interpolation options. Choose **Bicubic**, **Bilinear**, or **Nearest Neighbor**. In most cases, leave this option set at **Bicubic** for best results.

4 **Anti-alias PostScript check box:** This option ensures smooth results when placing or importing PostScript images.

5 **Export Clipboard check box:** This option attempts to export the current Clipboard contents when Photoshop is closed. Leave this option disabled because it slows the shutdown process and because the exported format is almost always incompatible.

6 **Short PANTONE Names check box:** Shortens Pantone names as they appear.

7 **Show ToolTips check box:** Activates the pop-up tool descriptions when you hover the mouse pointer over the interface elements.

8 **Auto-update open documents check box:** Updates and saves open documents automatically.

9 **Beep When Done check box:** Emits an audible beep when a task is complete.

10 **Dynamic Color Sliders check box:** Updates the current color selections in the **Color** palette in real time as the sliders are adjusted. Disable this check box for a slight performance increase.

11 **Save Palette Locations check box:** Reopens palettes in the same place and at the same size as they were when they were closed.

12 **Show Font Names in English check box:** Translates all font names into English.

13 **Reset Palette Locations to Default button:** Click to open all palettes and arrange them in their default locations.

Saving Files

Choose **File, Preferences, Saving Files** to launch the **Saving Files Preferences** dialog box. You use this dialog box to specify how a file is saved, including previews, thumbnails, and compatibility with files created in older versions of Photoshop.

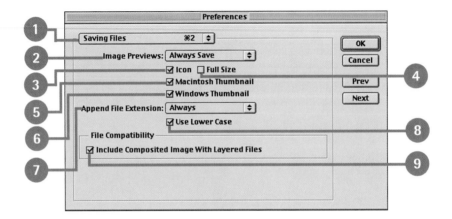

1. **Preferences Title pop-up menu:** Click the arrow to display a list of other pages in the **Preferences** dialog box; choose an option to open that page.

2. **Image Previews pop-up menu:** Click the arrow to display a list of save options and then choose one of these options: **Always Save, Never Save,** or **Ask When Saving.**

3. **Icon check box (Mac only):** Saves an icon preview for viewing within windows on the desktop.

4. **Full Size check box (Mac only):** Saves a 72 dpi file version for applications that can open only low-resolution Photoshop files.

5. **Macintosh Thumbnail check box (Mac only):** Creates a thumbnail to be displayed in the **Open** dialog box.

6. **Windows Thumbnail check box (Mac only):** Creates a thumbnail to be displayed in Windows systems.

7. **Append File Extension pop-up menu (Mac only):** Adds file extensions as a file is saved, based on the file format. Click the arrow to display a list: **Always, Never,** and **Ask When Saving.**

8. **Use Lower Case check box:** Adds the file extension using lowercase letters. In Windows, the **File Extension** drop-down list offers the choice between automatically adding extensions to filenames in **Upper Case** or **Lower Case** letters.

9. **Include Composited Image with Layered Files check box:** Adds a composited version of the file along with the layered version for compatibility with older versions of Photoshop that do not support layers.

Display & Cursors

Choose **File, Preferences, Display & Cursors** to open the **Preferences** dialog box to the **Display & Cursors** page. You use this dialog box to specify brush and cursor shapes and sizes.

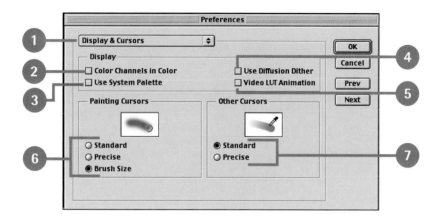

1 **Preferences Title pop-up menu:** Click the arrow to display a list of other pages in the **Preferences** dialog box; choose an option to open that page.

2 **Color Channels in Color check box:** Displays the color channels in color rather than in grayscale.

3 **Use System Palette check box:** Uses the system's standard 256-color palette for all dithering and 8-bit image displays.

4 **Use Diffusion Dither check box:** Employs a random dot pattern for dithering (which generally has a smoother result) instead of the default pattern dither.

5 **Video LUT Animation check box:** Controls image selection preview options using a third-party video card lookup table. Not relevant for most users and systems; leave this check box disabled unless you're sure that you need it.

6 **Painting Cursors radio buttons:** Enable you to select **Standard** (icon), **Precise** (cross hairs), or **Brush Size** (circular) for the painting cursor.

7 **Other Cursors radio buttons:** Enable you to select between a **Standard** (icon) and **Precise** (cross hairs) cursor.

Transparency & Gamut

Choose **File, Preferences, Transparency & Gamut** to open the **Preferences** dialog box to the **Transparency & Gamut** page. You use this dialog box to specify how transparency is shown in a file, as well as the gamut warning color format.

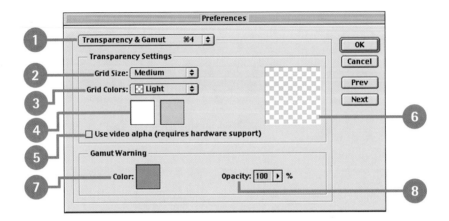

1. **Preferences Title pop-up menu:** Click the arrow to display a list of other pages in the **Preferences** dialog box; choose an option to open that page.

2. **Grid Size pop-up menu:** Controls the size of the checkerboard used to indicate transparency. Options are **None, Small, Medium,** and **Large**.

3. **Grid Colors pop-up menu:** Controls the color of the checkerboard used to indicate transparency. Options are **Light, Medium, Dark, Red, Orange, Green, Blue, Purple,** and **Custom**.

4. **Custom color swatches:** Click one or both of the swatches to select specific colors for the transparency checkerboard.

5. **Use video alpha check box:** Enables video alpha capability.

6. **Transparency preview window:** Shows the current checkerboard pattern.

7. **Gamut Warning Color swatch:** Click to display the **Color Picker** so that you can select the color that will show in place of the out-of-gamut color.

8. **Gamut Opacity slider:** Click and drag the slider to control the transparency of the color you've chosen to replace the out-of-gamut color.

Units & Rulers

Choose **File, Preferences, Units & Rulers** to open the **Preferences** dialog box to the **Units & Rulers** page. You use this dialog box to specify the format and measurements for rulers and columns.

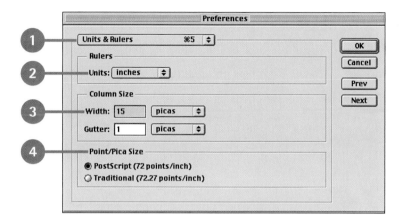

1 Preferences Title pop-up menu: Click the arrow to display a list of other pages in the **Preferences** dialog box; choose an option to open that page.

2 Rulers Units pop-up menu: Click the arrow to display a list of the units of measurement for Photoshop rulers. Options include **pixels**, **inches**, **centimeters**, **points**, **picas**, and **percent**.

3 Column Size Width and Gutter pop-up menus: Enter the width of a target column and the width of the *gutter* (the space between columns) for layout purposes. When resizing an image or canvas, the units you specify here are the ones you'll see in the **Resize** dialog box.

4 Point/Pica Size radio buttons: Select either the **PostScript** or the **Traditional** measurement system.

Guides & Grid

Choose **File, Preferences, Guides & Grid** to open the **Preferences** dialog box to the **Guides & Grid** page. You use this dialog box to control interpolation, the Color Picker option, and a number of other general application parameters.

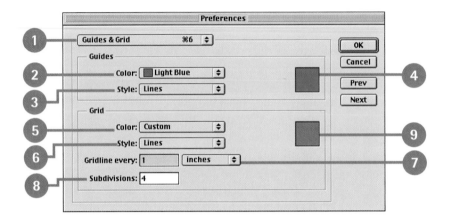

1   **Preferences Title pop-up menu:** Click the arrow to display a list of other pages in the **Preferences** dialog box; choose an option to open that page.

2   **Guides Color pop-up menu:** Select the color of the guide lines. Choices are **Light Blue, Light Red, Green, Medium Blue, Yellow, Magenta, Cyan, Light Gray, Black,** and **Custom.**

3   **Guides Style pop-up menu:** Determines the format of the guides. Options are solid **Lines** and **Dashed Lines.**

4   **Guides color swatch:** Click to open the **Color Picker** so that you can select a custom guide color.

5   **Grid Color pop-up menu:** Select the color of the grid. Choices are **Light Blue, Light Red, Green, Medium Blue, Yellow, Magenta, Cyan, Light Gray, Black,** and **Custom.**

6   **Grid Style pop-up menu:** Determines the format of the grid. Options are solid **Lines, Dots,** or **Dashed Lines.**

7 **Gridline controls:** Select the unit of measurement from the pop-up menu for the main grid divisions. Choices are **pixels, inches, centimeters, points, picas,** and **percent**. After you select a unit, type the number of units between gridlines.

8 **Subdivisions:** Determines how many subdivisions fall between each main gridline. Enter the desired value in the field.

9 **Grid color swatch:** Click to open the **Color Picker** so that you can select a custom grid color.

Plug-Ins & Scratch Disks

Choose **File, Preferences, Plug-Ins & Scratch Disks** to open the **Preferences** dialog box to the **Plug-Ins & Scratch Disks** page. You use this dialog box to tell Photoshop where to look for plug-ins and scratch disks.

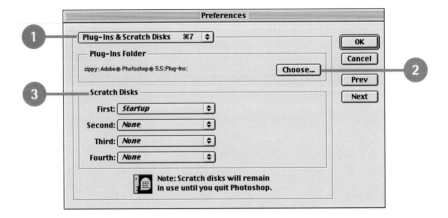

① **Preferences Title pop-up menu:** Click the arrow to display a list of other pages in the **Preferences** dialog box; choose an option to open that page.

② **Plug-Ins Folder Choose button:** Click to navigate to the Photoshop plug-ins folder. This folder usually is located in the Photoshop 5.5 application folder and is the folder in which you normally install your plug-ins.

③ **Scratch Disks pop-up menus:** Click to select up to four disks that will serve as scratch disks. All mounted disks are listed as scratch disk options. You may need more than one scratch disk if you work with particularly large image files.

Image Cache

Choose **File, Preferences, Image Cache** to open the **Preferences** dialog box to the **Image Cache** page. You use this dialog box to set the number of caching levels—a Photoshop method for speeding screen redraw.

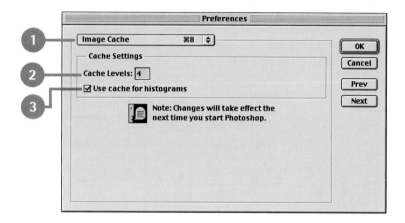

Preferences Title pop-up menu: Click the arrow to display a list of other pages in the **Preferences** dialog box; choose an option to open that page.

Cache Levels field: Enter the number of cache levels you want to use. A higher number speeds redraws but requires more RAM and can increase the time it takes to open an image.

Use cache for histograms check box: Enable this box to use image caching (using memory to temporarily hold information) for calculating histograms (graphs of the colors and brightness/darkness of an image).

Physical Memory Usage (Windows only): Set the amount of memory (in percentage of total memory) that you want to dedicate to Photoshop while it's running. The more memory you can give Photoshop, the better it will run. Keep in mind, however, that this setting may take memory away from other applications you may be running.

TASK *11*

How to Set ImageReady Preferences

General Controls

Choose **File, Preferences, General** to open the **Preferences** dialog box to the **General** page. You use this dialog box to control interpolation, the **Color Picker** option, and a number of other general application parameters.

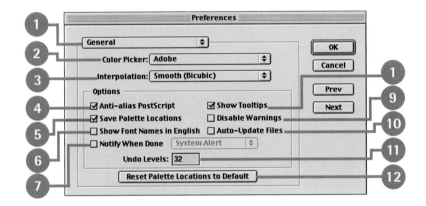

(1) **Preferences Title pop-up menu:** Click the arrow to display a list of other pages in the **Preferences** dialog box; choose an option to open that page.

(2) **Color Picker pop-up menu:** Click the arrow to display the list of options; then select the Adobe or Apple/Windows Color Picker.

(3) **Interpolation pop-up menu:** Click the arrow to display the list of options: **Smooth (Bicubic)**, **Bilinear**, and **Nearest Neighbor**. In most cases, leave this option set at **Smooth (Bicubic)** for best results.

(4) **Anti-alias PostScript check box:** Select this option to achieve smooth results when placing or importing PostScript images.

(5) **Save Palette Locations check box:** Reopens palettes in the same place and at the same size as when they were closed.

(6) **Show Font Names in English check box:** Translates all font names into English.

(7) **Notify When Done check box and pop-up menu:** Enable the check box to produce a notification when tasks are completed. Choose **System Alert** or **Text to Speech** from the pop-up menu as the notification method.

8 **Show ToolTips check box:** Activates the pop-up tool descriptions when you hover the mouse pointer over the interface elements.

9 **Disable Warnings check box:** Disables layer effect and selection warnings.

10 **Auto-Update Files check box:** Updates and saves files automatically.

11 **Undo Levels field:** Determines the number of undo states supported by the **History** palette. Enter a value in the field to change the setting. The higher you set this number, the more memory ImageReady uses to store the changes.

12 **Reset Palette Locations to Default button:** Click to open all palettes and arrange them in their default locations.

Saving Files

Choose **File, Preferences, Saving Files** to open the **Preferences** dialog box to the **Saving Files** page. You use this dialog box to specify the naming convention for slices and rollovers, as well as how and where automatically generated files are saved.

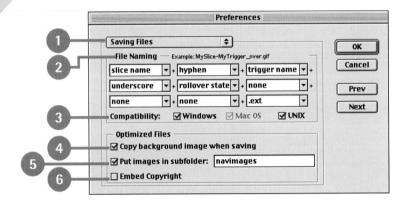

1 **Preferences Title pop-up menu:** Click the arrow to display a list of other pages in the **Preferences** dialog box; choose an option to open that page.

2 **File Naming drop-down menus:** Each of these nine drop-down menus enables you to specify a component in the naming protocol as slices and rollovers are created. The first eight menus include name, date, and numerical designations; the last menu offers an .EXT extension on the filename.

3 **Compatibility check boxes:** Enable the appropriate boxes to make files compatible with Windows, Mac OS, or UNIX. One option is always grayed out to reflect the native platform you're working on.

4 **Copy background image when saving check box:** Saves a copy of the background image to the Clipboard when you save a file.

5 **Put images in subfolder check box and field:** Moves images to a separate folder, which is created as the file is saved. Enter a name for the folder in the space provided. Use this option to keep your Web images separate from your HTML files.

6 **Embed Copyright check box:** Writes image copyright information to the HTML file that is saved with an image. This information can be used to track images on the Web and to provide proof of ownership.

Slices

Choose **File, Preferences, Slices** to open the **Preferences** dialog box to the **Slices** page. You use this dialog box to specify how ImageReady generates slices, including naming conventions, colors, and slice lines.

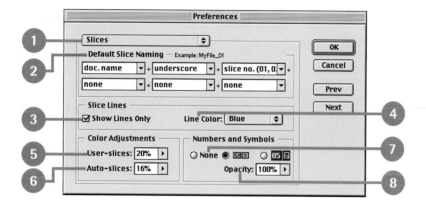

1   **Preferences Title pop-up menu:** Click the arrow to display a list of other pages in the **Preferences** dialog box; choose an option to open that page.

2   **Default Slice Naming drop-down menus:** Each of these six drop-down menus enables you to specify a component in the naming protocol for slices as you create them. Each menu includes name, date, and numerical designations.

3   **Show Lines Only check box:** Shows only the slice lines as slices are viewed, omitting the transparent coloring.

4   **Line Color pop-up menu:** Specifies the color of the slice lines. Choices include 24 color options.

5   **Color Adjustments User-slices box and slider:** Determines the opacity for user slices' color shading. Click the arrow and drag the slider or type a number value.

6   **Color Adjustments Auto-slices box and slider:** Determines the opacity for auto slices' color shading. Click the arrow and drag the slider or type a number value.

7   **Numbers and Symbols radio buttons:** Control the size of slice numbers and icons. Select **None** or the small or large icon button.

8   **Numbers and Symbols Opacity box and slider:** Click the arrow and drag the slider or type a number value to control the opacity of the slice numbers and symbols.

HTML

Choose **File, Preferences, HTML** to open the **Preferences** dialog box to the **HTML** page. You use this dialog box to specify how ImageReady writes HTML code as it builds tables and rollovers.

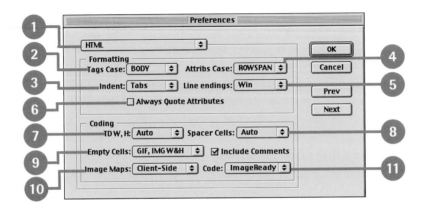

① **Preferences Title pop-up menu:** Click the arrow to display a list of other pages in the **Preferences** dialog box; choose an option to open that page.

② **Tags Case pop-up menu:** Determines the capitalization structure of tags. Choices are all caps, first-letter caps, or no caps.

③ **Indent pop-up menu:** Determines how indenting is handled as HTML is written. Choices are **Tabs, None, 1, 2, 4, 5,** and **8** spaces.

④ **Attribs Case pop-up menu:** Determines the capitalization structure of attributes. Choices are all caps, first-letter caps, midword caps, or no caps.

⑤ **Line endings pop-up menu:** Determines platform optimization. Choices are **Mac, Win,** and **UNIX.**

⑥ **Always Quote Attributes check box:** Places quotation marks around attributes.

⑦ **TD W, H pop-up menu:** Determines whether table data includes both width and height information. Choices are **Auto, Always,** and **Never.**

8   **Spacer Cells pop-up menu:** Determines whether spacer cells are used. Choices are **Auto**, **Always**, and **Never**.

9   **Empty Cells pop-up menu:** Determines the information used to fill empty cells. Choices are GIF image width and height, GIF table data width and height, and Nowrap table data width and height.

10   **Image Maps pop-up menu:** Determines how imagemaps are configured for client-side or server-side includes.

11   **Code pop-up menu:** Determines whether ImageReady or GoLive (a new WYSIWYG Web design program from Adobe) coding formats are used.

Optimization

Choose **File, Preferences, Optimization** to open the **Preferences** dialog box to the **Optimization** page. You use this dialog box to specify how optimization settings are calculated and displayed.

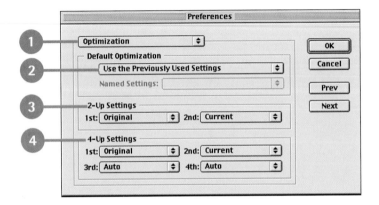

1 **Preferences Title pop-up menu:** Click the arrow to display a list of other pages in the **Preferences** dialog box; choose an option to open that page.

2 **Default Optimization pop-up menu:** Determines how optimization defaults are generated for an image. Choices are **Use the Previously Used Settings**, **Auto Select GIF/JPEG**, and **Use a Named Setting**.

3 **2-Up Settings pop-up menus:** Determine which iterations of the image are displayed in the 2-Up window. Defaults are **Original** and **Current**, but you also can choose from a long list of optimized presets.

4 **4-Up Settings pop-up menus:** Determine which iterations of the image are displayed in the 4-Up window. Defaults are **Original** and **Current**, but you also can choose from a long list of optimized presets, including **Auto**, which uses the next logical level of compression.

Cursors

Choose **File, Preferences, Cursors** to open the **Preferences** dialog box to the **Cursors** page. You use this dialog box to specify brush and cursor shapes and sizes.

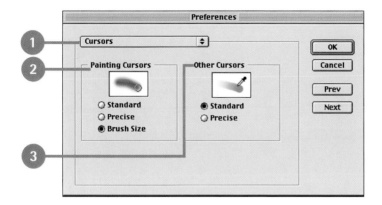

Preferences Title pop-up menu: Click the arrow to display a list of other pages in the **Preferences** dialog box; choose an option to open that page.

Painting Cursors radio buttons: Select **Standard** (icon), **Precise** (cross hairs), or **Brush Size** (circular) as the shape of the painting cursor.

Other Cursors radio buttons: Select between **Standard** (icon) and **Precise** (cross hairs) for the cursor shape.

Transparency

Choose **File, Preferences, Transparency** to open the **Preferences** dialog box to the **Transparency** page. You use this dialog box to specify how transparency is depicted in a file.

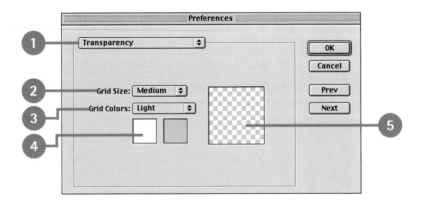

1 **Preferences Title pop-up menu:** Click the arrow to display a list of other pages in the **Preferences** dialog box; choose an option to open that page.

2 **Grid Size pop-up menu:** Controls the size of the checkerboard used to indicate transparency. Options are **None, Small, Medium,** and **Large.**

3 **Grid Colors pop-up menu:** Controls the color of the checkerboard used to indicate transparency. Options are **Light, Medium, Dark, Red, Orange, Green, Blue, Purple,** and **Custom.**

4 **Custom color swatches:** Click one or both of the swatches to select specific colors for the transparency checkerboard.

5 **Transparency preview window:** Shows the current transparency checkerboard pattern.

Plug-Ins & Scratch Disks

Choose **File, Preferences, Plug-Ins & Scratch Disks** to open the **Preferences** dialog box to the **Plug-Ins & Scratch Disks** page. You use this dialog box to tell ImageReady where to look for plug-ins and scratch disks.

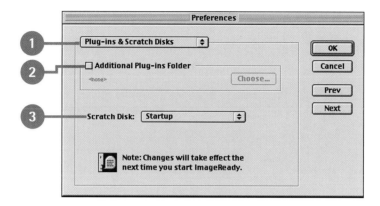

1 **Preferences Title pop-up menu:** Click the arrow to display a list of other pages in the **Preferences** dialog box; choose an option to open that page.

2 **Additional Plug-ins Folder check box and Choose button:** Enable the check box and click **Choose** to navigate to an additional plug-ins folder.

3 **Scratch Disk pop-up menu:** Click the arrow to display a list of potential scratch disks. All mounted disks are listed as scratch disk options.

Task

2

Optimizing Photoshop Projects

Although Photoshop often is thought of as a high-powered, creative tool, it is also a nuts-and-bolts production tool. Even though most designers would rather spend their time building montages and creative designs, they too often are saddled with less-glamorous tasks, such as cropping images and cataloging files.

The tasks in this part look at how to optimize your workflow, with tips and ideas on how to work faster and more efficiently. These tasks are valuable to master because you can apply them to other tasks, making everything you do a bit easier. In some situations, such as the tasks involving actions, these tips let you automate the entire process. Other tasks allow you to categorize groups of images into contact sheets, to share files, and to optimize the features in the **History** palette. ●

How to Build a Contact Sheet

A *contact sheet* is a Photoshop file with thumbnail references for all the images in a given folder. You can use contact sheets for a number of tasks, such as sending clients a list of images for approval, archiving, or just helping to organize your graphics visually rather than with archaic filenames. When you set up contact sheets, you have full control over the page size, the thumbnail size, and the spacing on the page. You can optimize the format of contact sheets for any printer or format.

Begin

1 Load Targets into a Single Folder

All the images for a contact sheet must reside in the same folder or subfolder. Drag the images into the target folder before you do anything else. This contact sheet will include all the images in the folder, so you should remove any image you don't want to appear on the contact sheet.

2 Choose Source Folder

To start building a contact sheet, choose **File, Automate, Contact Sheet II**. The **Contact Sheet** dialog box opens. In the **Source Folder** section, click the **Choose** button. Browse to the target folder (the folder containing the images), select it, and click **Open** to return to the main **Contact Sheet** dialog box.

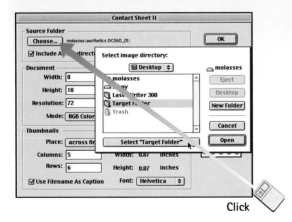

Click

3 Specify Size of Contact Sheet

In the **Document** area of the dialog box, specify the size of the contact sheet you're building. Enter the dimensions and resolution in the spaces provided. Keep the resolution at 72dpi if you're just viewing onscreen, or use a setting of 150dpi for basic-quality laser or inkjet printing. Watch the preview area on the right side of the dialog box change as you modify these values.

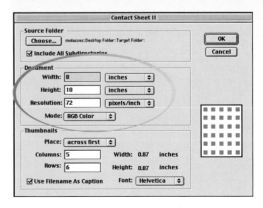

4 Set Color Mode

From the **Mode** drop-down list, select the color mode for your contact sheet: **RGB Color**, **CMYK Color**, **Lab Color**, or **Grayscale**. Make your choice based on the color modes of the images you're working with.

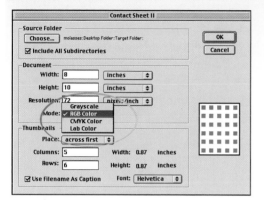

5 Determine Page Grid

Make a selection from the **Place** drop-down list and specify the numbers of **Columns** and **Rows** you want on your contact sheet. Watch the preview area to see how the values you provide affect the size of the thumbnails (based on the overall page dimensions).

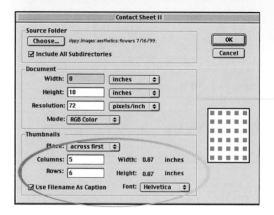

6 Set Captions and Fonts

Enable the **Use Filename as Caption** check box if you want the filenames of the images to appear below the thumbnails on the contact sheet. From the **Font** drop-down menu, select the font you want to use for the captions.

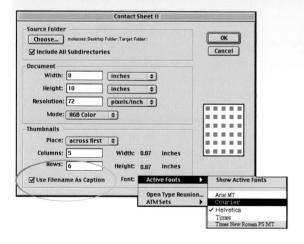

7 Build the Sheet

Click **OK** to start the script and build the contact sheet image. Note that the contact sheet is a Photoshop file; you can modify it any way you want. Consider saving the file as a .pdf file. This compact Adobe file format is especially suited for emailing to clients or if disk space is limited.

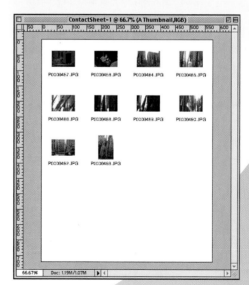

End

How to Move Files Between Illustrator and Photoshop

Adobe has done an excellent job of ensuring file compatibility among its major applications, including Go Live, PageMaker, and InDesign. If you take Photoshop and ImageReady as a group, the application you're most likely to share files with is Illustrator. This task is a collection of file-sharing options to help you move information between Illustrator's vector-based world and Photoshop's bitmap environment.

Begin

1 Create Compatible File Types

Although Photoshop accepts just about any type of graphics file, Illustrator is not so accommodating. Illustrator works only with Illustrator, Illustrator EPS, and Acrobat PDF files. Save your Photoshop files for use in Illustrator by choosing **File, Save As** and selecting one of the approved formats.

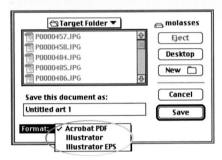

2 Export from Illustrator to Photoshop

With the file open in Illustrator, choose **File, Export** and rename the file. From the **Format** drop-down list, select **Photoshop 5** to save the file in Photoshop format. You then are asked to specify the color model and resolution.

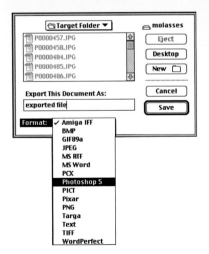

3 Drag Files Between Open Windows

One of the easiest ways to move files between applications is to open a window in both programs and drag the contents of one window to the other.

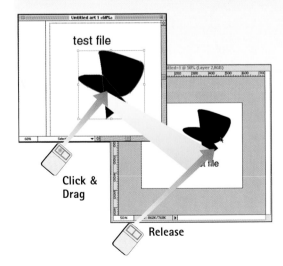

Click & Drag

Release

4 Copy and Paste

You also can copy and paste an image from one application to another. From either application, select the image and choose **Edit, Copy**. Activate the other application by clicking a toolbar or open window and then choose **Edit, Paste**. In Photoshop, you are asked to specify whether the file is being pasted as pixels or paths (Illustrator's files are scalable). In Illustrator, the file is a placed image based on the original file dimensions.

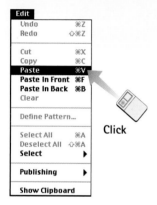

Click

5 Save Paths

When working with Photoshop and Illustrator, a powerful feature is having the programs share *paths,* the vector-based outlines used by both programs. Paths can be exported from Photoshop to Illustrator very smoothly; in Illustrator, you can then stroke or fill shape outlines for a number of graphical effects. In Photoshop, choose **File, Export Paths to Illustrator**. From the pop-up menu that appears, specify a filename that will contain the path. This action creates a new file containing only the path, which can then be opened in Illustrator.

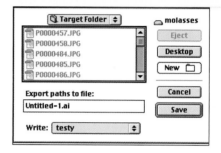

6 Drag Layers into Open Windows

You can drag the contents of a single layer between Photoshop and Illustrator. Select the layer from the **Layers** palette and drag it to an open Illustrator window. The contents of the selected layer appear automatically.

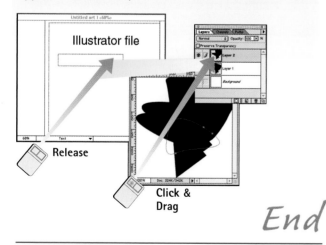

Illustrator file

Release

Click & Drag

How-To Hints

Preserve Illustrator Layers

When importing a file from Illustrator to Photoshop in Step 2, select the **Preserve Layers** option in the second dialog box to preserve the Illustrator layers when the file opens in Photoshop.

End

How to Use Multiple Views

People are working with larger images than ever before. One challenge is being able to zoom in on work at a pixel level while still monitoring the overall look of the piece. The best way to address this issue is by using *multiple views.* Just open two separate windows of the same file, specify a high rate of magnification for editing in one window, and leave the other at full screen size to check your progress as you work.

Begin

1 Open the Main File

Choose **File, Open** to display the **Open** dialog box. Select the file you want to work on and click **OK**.

Click

2 Set Desired Magnification

Click the **Zoom** tool in the toolbar and click the image. Watch the zoom percentage numbers in the lower left corner of the screen. Continue clicking to zoom in to the magnification level that lets you see the area clearly. To zoom in on a particular area of the image, click the **Zoom** tool and drag to draw a marquee around the area you want to magnify.

Click

3 Open a New View

To create a second window on this same image, choose **View, New View.** You now have two windows of the same image open on your desktop: One shows the full image, and the other shows a detailed zoom of a single area. At this point, you can create additional views for as many areas as necessary. (Don't worry about "using up" system resources when using multiple views; your computer can handle it!)

4 Drag Windows into Position

Because the active window automatically moves to the top of the desktop, you should arrange the image windows so that they are side by side. This arrangement allows you to see both the zoomed screen and the full screen at the same time.

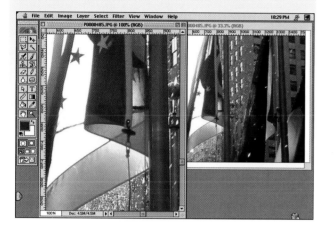

5 Edit the Image

Make any local edits to the image in either window. For example, you can paint, erase, or silhouette. (These and other tasks are explained later in this book.) As you work in one window, notice that the image is updated in real time in the other window.

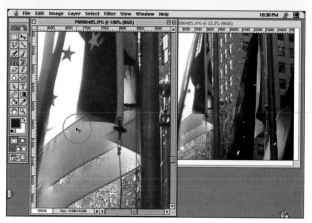

6 Reduce Number of Views

When you finish editing the image, close either of the view windows (click the **Close box** in the menu bar) to revert to a single view and reduce onscreen clutter.

How-To Hints

Use Macro and Micro Views

When necessary, open a third window to show a high magnification, normal size, and reduced view.

Zooming Shortcuts

Rather than selecting and deselecting the **Zoom** tool, you can temporarily change the current tool to the **Zoom** tool by pressing ⌘++ (Windows users press **Ctrl++**) to zoom in or ⌘+- (Windows users press **Ctrl+-**) to zoom out. Here's another tip: Hold the **spacebar** to temporarily convert whatever tool you're using to the **Hand** tool.

End

How to Undo with the History Palette

The **History** palette is one of the most powerful new features in Photoshop 5.0. It answers users' requests to build in some sort of multiple undo capability. Now you can revert an image back beyond the simple **Edit, Undo** command. The **History** palette records each edit or command as a *layer tile.* Click a tile to revert the image back to that previous state. You can set features and options to optimize how the **History** palette works for you.

Begin

1 Open the History Palette

Choose **Window, Show History** to open the **History** palette. The palette shows a snapshot at the top, representing the original state of the file as it was opened. As you make changes to the file, those changes are displayed as tiles running in descending order in the palette.

2 Set the Number of History States

Click and hold the black arrow in the upper-right corner of the palette to access the History palette menu. Drag down to select **History Options**; the **History Options** dialog box opens. Set the number of states you want to record; understand that any states that exceed this limit will be lost. If you set **Maximum History States** to **20**, for example, you cannot go back to what you did 21 steps ago. On the other hand, more states are memory intensive, so you must strike a happy medium between a **History** palette safety net and efficient allocation of memory and disk space.

Click

3 Take Snapshots

Another way to preserve a specific image state is to take a snapshot. Snapshots are independent of the standard image states mentioned in Step 2 and remain active until you close or save the file. To take a snapshot, display the **History** palette menu and select **New Snapshot**. Give the snapshot a name in the dialog box that appears and click **OK**. A thumbnail of the snapshot appears in the upper part of the palette.

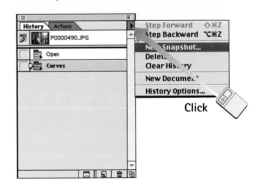

Click

4 Revert to a Previous State

To revert to a previous state or snapshot, select the corresponding tile in the **History** palette. The image in the active window reverts to the point in the editing process you selected. All tiles below the active tile dim, but you still can revert to them by clicking them.

Click

5 Create Duplicate Files

The **History** palette also lets you create a duplicate image file. After you create a duplicate, you can continue editing the duplicate, leaving the original in its previous state. To make a duplicate, choose **New Document** from the History palette menu. Photoshop copies the image in a new window, which you can modify further or rename and save.

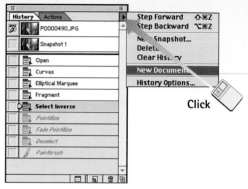

Click

End

How-To Hints

Watch Those Brushstrokes

Remember that each time you click the mouse to apply a brushstroke, you "consume" a history state. Clicking away with multiple brushstrokes can consume all your history states in a hurry. Be sure to grab a snapshot before you start brushing, leaving you an escape route to a previous version.

Use the History Brush

You also can do great things with the Photoshop **History** brush, which allows you to brush in corrections using history states as a source. See Part 8, Task 4, "How to Use the History Brush," for details.

TASK 5

How to Use the Preset Actions

Photoshop uses preset scripts called *actions* to automate repetitive tasks. For example, creating a drop shadow can involve inverting a selection, deleting a background, inverting the selection again, offsetting it, feathering it, and filling it with a transparent fill. Actions allow you to apply multiple steps such as these with a single mouse click. Actions can save you time—especially when you are processing multiple images in the same way. You can view actions in a simplified button mode (which allows for one-click application) and in a more detailed mode (in which you can examine each step in the action). In this task, you work in simplified **Button** mode. You'll get more detailed information in the following tasks.

Begin

1 Open the Actions Palette

Choose **Window, Show Actions** to open the **Actions** palette.

Click

2 Set Palette to Button Mode

Click and hold the arrow in the upper-right corner of the palette and drag down to select **Button Mode**. The **Actions** palette changes to display all the available actions as clickable buttons. Select this option again to disable **Button** mode and return the palette to the simple **List** mode.

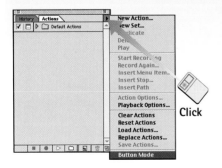

Click

3 Select an Area of the Image

Actions can be applied to a selected area of the image; in many cases, actions can be applied to the entire image. Click the **Marquee** tool and drag to select the area of the image you want to modify with an action.

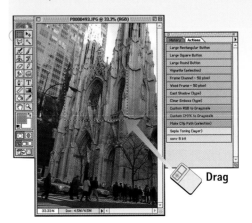

Drag

56 PART 2: OPTIMIZING PHOTOSHOP PROJECTS

4 Click the Action Button

Click the desired action button in the **Actions** palette to execute the effect. You can apply multiple actions to the same selection—just click another Action button.

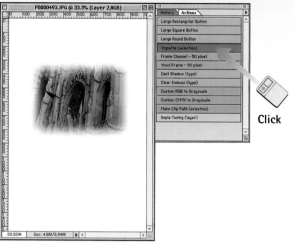

Click

End

How-To Hints

Keystroke Applications

If you deselect **Button Mode** from the Actions palette menu, you can set custom keystrokes for each action. For example, instead of going to the **Actions** palette to click the **Vignette** button, you could assign a keystroke such as **Shift+Ctrl+F2** that executes the Vignette action. In the **Actions** palette, select the action you want; open the palette menu and drag down to select **Action Options**. In the dialog box that opens, specify a keystroke to launch the action.

How to Create Custom Actions

Although some of the preset actions that ship with Photoshop are useful, the list as a whole is somewhat limited. It won't be long before you'll feel the need to build your own actions. An action should be generic enough to work in a number of situations and on multiple images. There may be some editing tasks that just don't translate into actions. Keep trying though, because building a clean action can give you a great deal of satisfaction, as well as save you a lot of time.

Begin

1 Open the Actions Palette

If the **Actions** palette is not currently displayed on your desktop, choose **Window, Show Actions** to display the palette. If necessary, exit **Button** mode and return the palette to **List** mode (see Step 2 in Task 5).

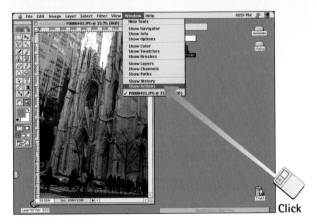

Click

2 Create a New Action

From the palette menu, select **New Action** to open the **New Action** dialog box. Type a name for the action you are going to record and select the **Set** orientation. (You can create multiple sets of actions, which you would then select from the **Set** menu. If no other sets of actions are created, select from the **Default Actions** set that appears.

Click

3 Execute the Action

Click the **Record** button to begin recording the action. The **New Action** dialog box disappears to give you free access to your desktop. In this example, I convert a file to grayscale, change it to index color, and invert it to create a negative image.

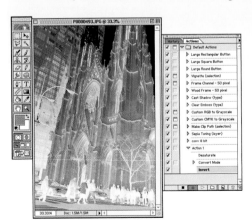

4 Select Stop Recording

After you perform all the steps of the action you want to record, choose **Stop Recording** from the palette menu to end the recording process.

Click

5 Action Sequence in the Palette

Go to the **Actions** palette and find your newly created action in the list. Click the right-facing arrow to display the list of steps you recorded for that action.

6 Add Any Missing Steps

If necessary, you can add steps by selecting a step as an insertion point (here I selected **Convert Mode**) and then selecting **Insert Menu Item** from the palette menu. Then type the name of the command as desired; Photoshop automatically records it and adds it to the action sequence *following* the selection. You also can select **Start Recording** and execute the commands to add steps.

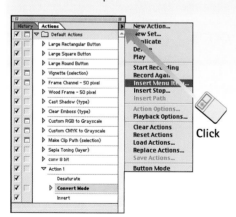

Click

End

How to Set Up Batch Processing Options

As described in the preceding tasks, actions allow you to apply multiple commands to one image with a single mouse click. But what do you do if you have a folder of 200 image files that all need the same action? Although you can open each image file and apply the action, it would be much better to process all 200 images with just a single command. This is what the Photoshop **Batch** command does. The process involves specifying a target folder that contains all the images to be processed, and then detailing how and where Photoshop saves the images created by the action.

Begin

1 Open the Actions Palette

If the **Actions** palette is not currently displayed on your desktop, choose **Window, Show Actions** to display the palette. If necessary, exit **Button** mode and return the palette to **List** mode (see Step 2 in Task 5).

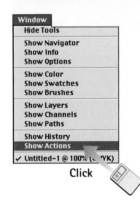

Click

2 Highlight the Action to Be Applied

In the **Actions** palette, click the action to be applied; the action is highlighted in the list. Ideally, you create the action first (refer to Task 6) and then you select that action for the **Batch** command to use when it processes the files.

Click

3 Open the Batch Dialog Box

From the menu bar, choose **File, Automate, Batch**. The **Batch** dialog box opens. The action you highlighted in Step 2 appears in the **Play** section.

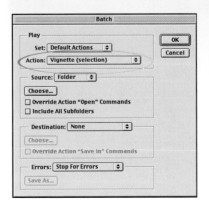

4 Select the Source Folder

From the **Source** drop-down list, select the **Folder** option and then click the **Choose** button. In the **Select the Batch Source Folder** dialog box that appears, navigate to highlight the folder containing the images you want to process and click the **Select** button. Back in the **Source** section, choose options if you want to process images in subfolders.

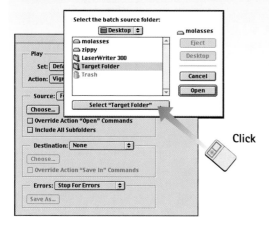

Click

5 Select the Destination Folder

Now specify where you want the changed images to be stored. From the **Destination** drop-down list, choose **None** (the changed images remain open onscreen), **Save and Close** (the changed images are saved and stored in their original location), or **Folder** (you then click the **Choose** button and navigate to the folder in which you want copies of the changed images to be stored).

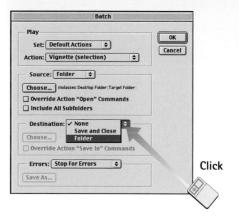

Click

6 Specify Error Handling

From the **Errors** drop-down list, select **Stop for Errors** (the process stops until errors are resolved) or **Log Errors to File** (the process continues and a list of errors is generated for later review). Click **OK** to begin running the selected action on the selected folders and subfolders.

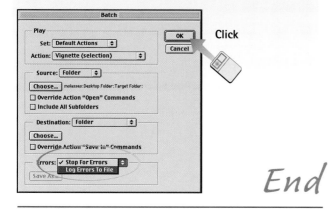

Click

End

How-To Hints

The Open and Save Commands

The **Batch** dialog box lets you designate special handling for opening and saving files. In many cases, individual actions include an **Open** command for a specific file, or a **Save** or **Save As** command that stores files in a unique place.

Because these specific commands could conflict with processing a whole folder of different images, Photoshop lets you override a specific "Open" command in an action with a generic one that opens each image in the folder, regardless of how it is named. In a similar manner, the override "Save in" command stores each file in the folder specified, rather than in a unique place as specified in the action.

Task

Selection Techniques

There are times when you need to change just a portion of an image rather than make global changes. To do this effectively, you usually select just the portion of the image you want to change, isolating it from the rest of the image. Then you can use all of Photoshop's editing tools to change just the selected area, leaving the remaining image unchanged.

As you select objects or areas in an image, it is important to take the time to select those areas as accurately as possible. Selections that include fringe elements from the background or that have poorly defined edges can destroy the realism and professional look of an image.

Photoshop goes to great lengths to provide a wide array of selection tools. This part provides a solid overview of the different kinds of selections you can make in Photoshop, as well as how to modify, combine, and save selections after you've made them. The Photoshop selection tools let you isolate just about any kind of image area; it is well worth your time to learn as much as you can about image selections. ●

How to Select Geometric Areas

Selecting geometric areas such as circles, ovals, and rectangles is a common Photoshop task. Reasons for selecting geometric areas include lightening an area to place text on it, deleting a section of the image, or preparing to crop the image.

Begin

1 Open the File

Choose **File, Open** to open the desired file.

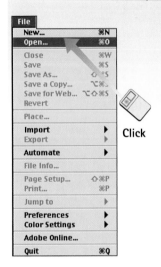

Click

2 Select the Marquee Tool

Select the **Rectangular Marquee** tool to draw a rectangular selection; select the **Elliptical Marquee** tool to draw an oval selection. To select the **Elliptical Marquee** tool, click and hold the **Marquee** tool and drag to the desired tool in the pop-out menu that appears.

Rectangle   Elliptical
Marquee   Marquee

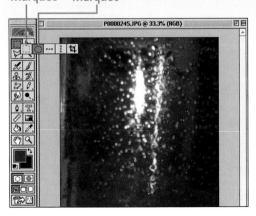

3 Drag the Selection

Move the cursor onto the image and click and drag to draw the selection. If the selection is not where you want it, click once outside the selection to deselect the area, and drag to redraw the selection.

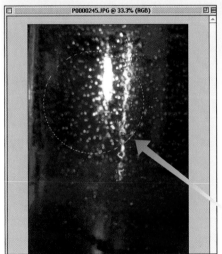

Drag

4 Move the Selection as Needed

After you create the selection, you can move it to another area in the image. With the **Rectangular Marquee** or **Elliptical Marquee** tool still selected, click inside the active selection and drag to move its location.

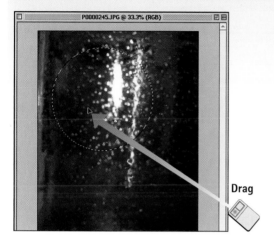

Drag

5 Deselect as Necessary

If you need to deselect the area and start over, choose **Select, Deselect** to deactivate the current selection. You also can deactivate a selection by clicking outside the selected area or by pressing ⌘+D (Mac users) or **Ctrl+D** (Windows users) when using any of the marquee tools.

Click

End

How-To Hints

Select a Specific Size

To make a selection of a specific size, double-click the **Marquee** tool to launch the **Marquee Options** palette. Choose **Fixed Size** from the **Style** drop-down list and enter the dimensions in the **Height** and **Width** fields. Click in the image to create a selection matching the dimensions you entered.

Select a Size Ratio

To select a perfect circle or square, press and hold the **Shift** key as you drag the selection. To constrain any other size ratio (that is, to drag a selection area that preserves a height/width ratio), select **Constrained Aspect Ratio** from the **Style** drop-down list in the **Marquee Options** palette and type values for the desired width-to-height ratio.

Draw from the Center Out

To draw a selection from the center out instead of from a corner down, hold the **Option** key (Mac users) or **Alt** key (Windows users) as you drag.

How to Use the Polygonal Lasso Tool

The **Polygonal Lasso** tool lets you create selections with straight-line segments so that you can create complex geometric areas such as starbursts and objects in perspective. It does not let you create curved segments, however, so make sure that your selection area is suited for this tool.

Begin

1 Open the File

Choose **File, Open** and select the desired file.

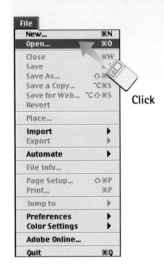

Click

2 Select the Polygonal Lasso Tool

Click and hold the **Lasso** tool in the toolbar and drag to select the **Polygonal Lasso** tool from the pop-out menu that appears.

3 Click the First Point

Move the pointer onto the image and click to place the first anchor point. After placing the first point, notice that a straight line extends between the anchor point and the cursor. This line indicates the selection line that will be created when you click to place another anchor point.

Click

4 Add Other Points as Needed

Click once at each location on the image and place as many anchor points as necessary to surround the area you are selecting.

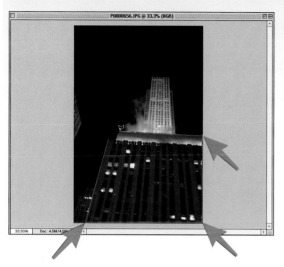

5 Close the Selection

To define an enclosed area, you can close the selection shape by clicking back on the starting anchor point. Alternatively, you can either double-click or ⌘+click (Mac users) or **Ctrl**+click (Windows users) to connect the current point to the starting point. When you do this, the selection process is complete.

Click

End

How-To Hints

Use the Shift Key for Right Angles

Press and hold the **Shift** key to constrain the line segments you draw with the **Polygonal Lasso** tool to right angles.

For Organic Selections

Select the **Lasso** tool instead of the **Polygonal Lasso** tool to draw free-form shape selections. You can switch to the **Lasso** tool from the **Polygonal Lasso** tool on-the-fly by pressing and holding the **Option** key (Mac users) or **Alt** key (Windows users) as you drag free-form shapes. Release the **Option/Alt** key to go back to dragging straight lines.

How to Select by Color Range

When the area you want to select is predominantly one color, think about using the color range as a selection criterion. This approach selects all the pixels in an image based on a specified color value. The color-range controls let you designate the exact range so that you can fine-tune the selection to a specific set of colors.

Begin

1 Open the File

Choose **File, Open** to launch the desired file.

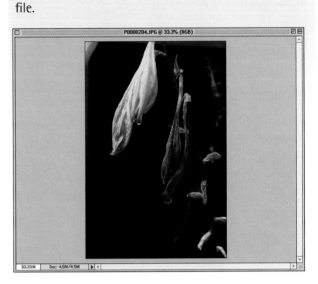

2 Select the Color Range Command

Choose **Select, Color Range** to launch the **Color Range** dialog box.

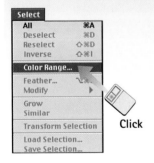

3 Configure the Dialog Box

Click the arrow to the right of the **Select** option and drag to select **Sampled Colors**. Start with the **Fuzziness** slider set to **40**, choose the **Selection** radio button, and set the **Selection Preview** option to **None**.

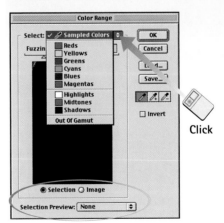

4 Sample a Color

Move the cursor onto the image; notice that the cursor changes to an eyedropper as it moves over the image. Click on a color you want to select. In this example, I clicked to select the purple in the flower; the preview in the dialog box shows how much of the image has that color. You can control how much variation of that color is selected by adjusting the **Fuzziness** slider.

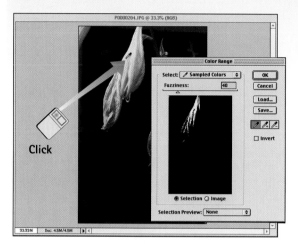

5 Adjust the Fuzziness Slider

Increase or decrease the **Fuzziness** slider to include more or less of the color in the selection. Choose the **Black Matte** and **White Matte** options in the **Selection Preview** list in the **Color Range** dialog box to evaluate the selection area.

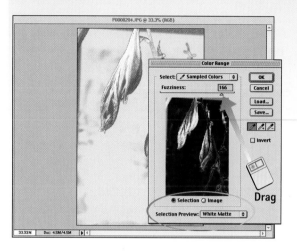

6 Add Additional Colors

Select the **Plus Eyedropper** from the dialog box and click on the image to add additional colors to the selected range. Click **OK** to close the dialog box and make the selection. If the selection is not to your satisfaction, adjust the **Fuzziness** slider and try again.

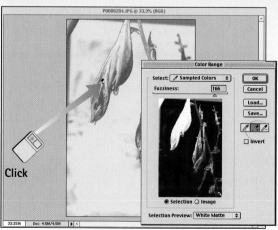

End

How-To Hints

Image Previews

To check the selection in more detail, select **Grayscale**, **Black Matte**, **White Matte**, or **Quick Mask** from the **Selection Preview** drop-down list to show the selection results in the main image window. **Grayscale** shows selected areas in white and unselected areas in black. **Black Matte** shows selected areas as normal and unselected areas as flat black. **White Matte** shows selected areas as normal and unselected areas as white. **Quick Mask** places a mask over the selected or unselected areas, depending on how the **Quick Mask Options** are set (see the following task for details). To select all of a particular color or tonal range in an image, choose the desired color from the **Select** drop-down list. You also can select **Out of Gamut** to show which colors would be lost in an RGB-to-CMYK file conversion.

How to Use Quick Mask

Quick Mask is an intuitive way of selecting complex image areas using Photoshop's paint tools to define the selection area. The area is painted in as a mask, and you can erase or add to the mask to define the exact area you want to select. After you define the area, you exit Quick Mask to select the area. When you use Quick Mask with Photoshop's other painting tools (such as the **Paintbrush** tool), you can literally "paint" a mask or selection using the actual image as a guideline. In fact, you won't need to worry about staying within the lines because you can easily reverse the painting by switching the color you're painting with.

1 Open the File

Choose **File, Open** to launch the desired file.

2 Make a Basic Selection

Although you can start the selection process with Quick Mask, I find it is easier to make an initial selection first, just to set up a relationship between the mask and the rest of the image. Use any of Photoshop's selection tools and select the general area you want to define. Here, I used the **Magic Wand** tool to select a portion of the statue's back.

3 Set Quick Mask Options

Double-click the **Quick Mask** button in the toolbox to launch the **Quick Mask Options** dialog box. Select **Masked Areas** or **Selected Areas** to specify whether the mask represents the selection or the background (that is, whether you are covering or uncovering as you paint the mask). The default mask color is red, but you can click the color swatch and select another color. The selection you made in Step 2 reflects these settings as you make them. When everything looks good, click **OK**.

Double-click

4 Draw or Paint the Selection

Use the Photoshop paint tools to fine-tune the mask. See Part 8, "Drawing, Painting, and Filling with Color," for details. You can choose smaller or larger brushes or zoom in to follow the lines of your image more closely. As you'll see in the next task, you also can easily erase any areas where you "painted" outside the lines.

5 Erase Unwanted Areas

Select the **Erase** tool and erase the mask to reduce the selection area as necessary.

Erase tool

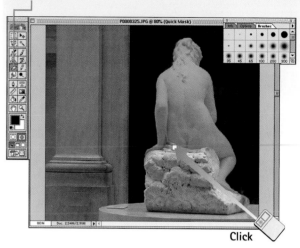

Click

6 Exit Quick Mask

Click the **Standard Mode** button in the toolbox to exit Quick Mask and convert the mask to a selection. Alternatively, press the **Q** key to toggle between standard mode and Quick Mask mode to make sure that the selection is correct for the work you're doing to the image.

End

How-To Hints

Filter Quick Mask for Graphic Effects

While still in Quick Mask mode, you can use any of Photoshop's filters to apply unique textures to the mask. When you switch to standard mode, the texture of the selection is reflected as you edit the image.

Use the Type Tool for Text Selections

While in Quick Mask mode, you also can use the **Type Mask** tool to create text selections. Fill the selections with the mask to make the selection active, and then modify the selection further with filters or other tools.

How to Select Areas Using Paths

Because paths define the edges of an area, it's only natural that you use them to create a selection. Paths are a good selection choice if you need to select areas with smooth, flowing curves and precise angles. Because Part 10, "Using Paths," goes to great lengths to describe how to work with paths, this task focuses only on how to convert a path to a selection.

Begin

1 Open the File

Choose **File, Open** to launch the desired file.

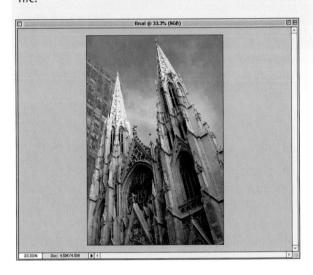

2 Select the Pen Tool

Select the **Pen** tool from the toolbox.

Click

3 Draw a Path or Segment

Starting at one side of the area you want to select, click the **Pen** tool on the image to create the necessary points for a path or segment. (A *segment* is a path that has not been joined at both ends.) You are trying to create a contained area. In this example, I have selected the steeples, but note that the selection path runs off both edges of the image area.

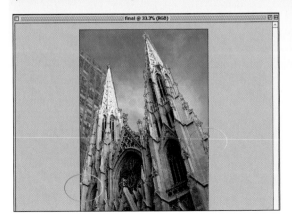

4 Make the Path a Selection

Choose **Window, Show Paths** to launch the **Paths** palette. From the palette menu, select **Make Selection** to launch the **Make Selection** dialog box. Select the **Feather Radius** and **Anti Alias** options if you want to soften the selection, and click **OK.** The segmented path line now includes a blinking selection line. If you did not define a contained area in Step 3, Photoshop joins your first and last points to "complete" the selection area.

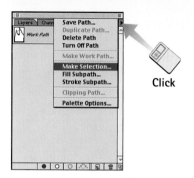

Click

5 Deselect the Path

At this point, both the path and the selection are active. In the **Paths** palette, deselect the path tile so that only the selection is active.

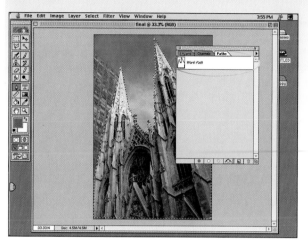

End

How-To Hints

Use Paths Instead of Saving Selections

Paths are a smart alternative to saving selections because paths add very little to the file size and can be infinitely modified and resized. Selections are saved as channels, which can bloat overall file size very quickly.

How to Modify Selections

To select complex shapes and areas, you must sometimes combine multiple selection methods. Adding or subtracting from a selection is only the beginning. You also can shrink or grow a selection, smooth sharp corners, and tweak or skew the selection area in any direction. This task shows the top 12 shortcuts for working with selections. Combine them as you see fit to select exactly the right area of your image.

Begin

1 Adding to Selections

To add to a selection, hold the **Shift** key as you're using any of the Photoshop selection tools. A plus sign appears next to the cursor to show that you're adding to the current selection.

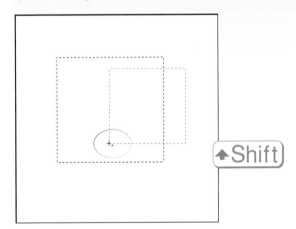

2 Subtracting from Selections

To subtract from a selection, hold the **Option** key (Mac users) or **Alt** (Windows users) as you're using any of the Photoshop selection tools. A minus sign appears next to the cursor to show that you're subtracting from the current selection.

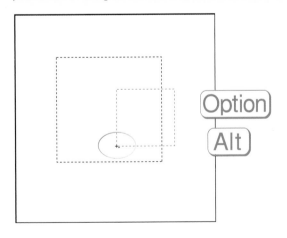

3 Intersecting Selections

With an area selected, it is possible to create a second, overlapping area that leaves only the common, intersecting area selected. First, select an area. Then press **Shift+Option** (Mac users) or **Shift+Alt** (Windows users) as you draw a second selection that overlaps the first. An + appears next to the cursor as you do this. After you release the mouse and the keyboard keys, only the intersecting area remains selected.

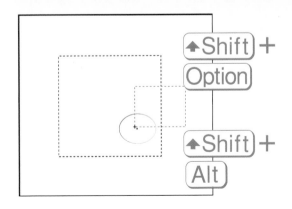

4 Nudging a Selection

After you select an area, you can nudge the selection area up, down, left, or right one pixel at a time. Select one of the **Marquee** tools in the toolbox and press the arrow keys on your keyboard.

5 Inverting Selections

To invert an active selection, choose **Select, Inverse**. This action selects the exact opposite of the current selection. In this example, after you select the menu command, everything on the image area *except* the rectangle currently selected will be selected.

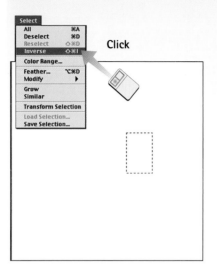

6 Smoothing Selections

Smoothing a selection involves a gradual rounding of corners or sharp edges. To smooth an active selection, choose **Select, Modify, Smooth**. In the **Smooth Selection** dialog box that appears, enter a value from 1 to 16 pixels to determine the degree of smoothing. Click **OK** to modify the selection.

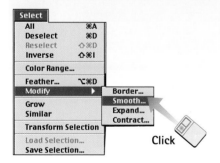

7 Expanding Selections

Expanding a selection does just what it says: expands the overall area of a selection by a specific number of pixels. To expand an active selection, choose **Select, Modify, Expand**. In the **Expand Selection** dialog box that appears, enter a value from 1 to 16 pixels to determine the degree of expansion. Click **OK** to modify the selection.

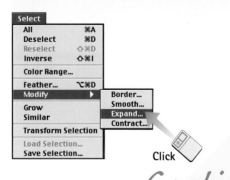

Continues

8 Contracting Selections

Contracting a selection makes the overall selection area smaller. To contract an active selection, choose **Select, Modify, Contract**. In the **Contract Selection** dialog box that appears, enter a value from 1 to 16 pixels. Click **OK** to modify the selection.

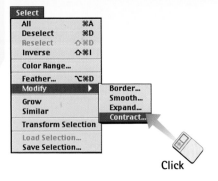

Click

9 Isolating Selection Borders

When working with geometric selections, there may be times when you want to apply an effect only to the *border* of a selected area. Choose **Select, Modify, Border**. In the **Border** dialog box that appears, enter a value from 1 to 16 pixels to specify the width of the border. This option thickens the selection line to the width you specify and makes that border line the active selection area. Click **OK** to modify the selection.

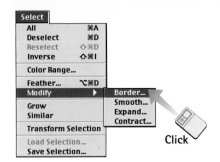

Click

10 Feathering a Selection

Feathering a selection involves softening the selection edges, vignetting (softening) any effects that are applied to the selected area. To feather a selection, choose **Select, Feather**. In the **Feather Selection** dialog box that appears, enter a feather value from 0.2 pixels to 250 pixels and click **OK**.

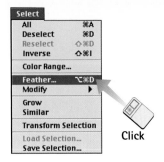

Click

11 Selecting Similar Colors

After you select an area, you can select all other pixels in the image that have the same color value. This capability can be effective if you want to select multiple colored objects or areas. To do this, select a color or range of colors, and then choose **Select, Similar**. All pixels with similar pixel values then are selected.

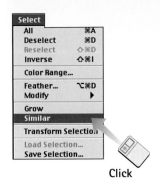

Click

12 Transforming Selections

You can distort or skew a selection using any of the **Transform** options described in Part 11, Task 3, "How to Transform Layers." To transform an active selection, choose **Select, Transform Selection**. A bounding box appears around the selection; drag the handles to modify the selection area.

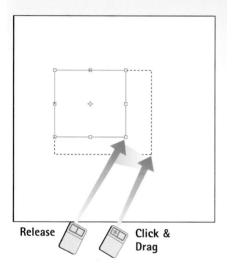

Release   Click & Drag

End

How-To Hints

Smooth Selections to Make Rounded Corners

Use the **Smooth Selection** technique from Step 6 to create rounded-corner rectangular selections. The 16-pixel rounding value works very well with 72dpi Web images. The result is ready to be stroked or filled to create a rounded-corner box shape.

Use Tolerance with Select Similar

The **Select Similar** command in Step 11 uses the tolerance setting from the **Magic Wand** options palette to determine how it selects similar colors. If you set the tolerance high, more "similar" colors are selected; if you set the tolerance low, a more narrow range of colors is selected.

TASK

How to Save and Load Selections

After you've gone to the trouble of making the perfect selection, you may want to save that selection for future use. This is especially true if you've selected an object or area you know you're going to be going back to as you work with the image. Photoshop lets you save selections as *alpha channels*, which preserve the exact area and transparency levels and can be reloaded at any time.

Begin

1 Open the File

Choose **File, Open** and launch the desired file.

2 Make the Selection

Select the desired area using any of Photoshop's selection tools. In this example, I used the **Color Range** dialog box to select the green blades of grass.

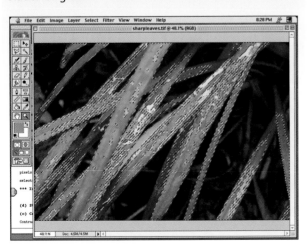

3 Choose Save Selection

Choose **Select, Save Selection**. The **Save Selection** dialog box opens.

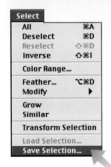

Click

4 Name the Selection Channel

In the **Name** field, type a name for the selection. This is the name Photoshop gives to the alpha channel, which is where the selection is saved. Click **OK** to save the selection.

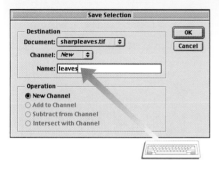

5 Load the Selection

To load a saved selection, choose **Select, Load Selection**. In the **Save Selection** dialog box that appears, choose the selection name from the **Channel** drop-down list and click **OK** to activate the selection. Note that you can load a selection from any open document.

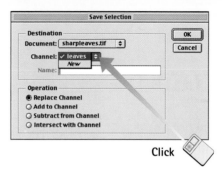

Click

End

How-To Hints

PSD or TIFF?

To preserve the channel along with the saved file in Step 4, you must use either the native Photoshop format (**.PSD**) or the TIFF format. The PSD format is safest, though, and can hold more than one extra channel.

View Saved Selections

All saved selections are visible in the **Channels** palette, listed by the name you entered in Step 4. To review saved selections, choose **Window, Show Channels** to open the **Channels** palette and examine all saved selections.

File Size Caution

Although saving selections is easy and convenient, these selections can dramatically increase file size if you're not careful. This is especially true if you're saving multiple selections in one file, if your selections are large, or if they include transparent areas. To monitor file size as you work, choose **Document Sizes** from the pop-up menu on the status bar at the bottom of the image window. The value on the left shows the current image's file size if the image were to be flattened; the value on the right shows the image's file size saved with any additional layers and channels.

Task

4

Converting Files

*T*he tasks in this part walk you through the various processes for saving, converting, and optimizing files. Knowing how to convert files is important; you don't have to work in graphics very long before someone calls to tell you that they can't read the file you just sent them. There are lots of different file formats, ranging from TIFF, JPEG, and EPS down to the obscure formats, such as Amiga HAM and Scitex CT.

File formats evolved over time in an environment where there were no standards. Therefore, many files are compatible; you'll find that TIFF, PICT, BMP, and other formats are interchangeable as far as pragmatic functionality is concerned. Some systems require specific formats (such as Amiga and Scitex), so you can easily figure out when to employ those options.

Adding to this confusion is the discrepancy between Mac and Windows platforms as well as issues around transferring files between Windows 95, Windows 98, and Windows NT. With all these different systems and platforms, it's a wonder anything gets transferred successfully.

In addition to pure file conversions, it is also important to *optimize* files for use in different capacities, such as prepping files for print or building compact Web files. Optimizing files involves striking a balance among image clarity, proper color modes, and file size.

Fortunately, Photoshop excels in the realm of file conversion. Before it was an image-editing program, Photoshop's core technology was in file conversion. That's why there are almost 20 file formats available in the Photoshop **Save As** dialog box. For optimization, you will find the same optimize capabilities in both Photoshop 5.5 and ImageReady 2.0. Choosing **File, Save for Web** in Photoshop opens a comparison dialog box that delivers the same kind of optimization control as ImageReady's **Optimize** palette. Unless stated otherwise, the file optimization methods given in these parts work in either program. ●

How to Save Files in Other Formats

At first glance, changing a file's format can be a confusing and complicated matter, especially if you don't know what all those acronyms stand for. The reality is that it's not as complicated as it first appears. Photoshop provides almost 20 format options to choose from; all you have to do is know which ones to use.

Begin

1 Flatten the Image

With your image open in Photoshop you can, if necessary, *flatten* any layers. Open the **Layers** palette (choose **Window, Show Layers**). Click and hold the triangle in the upper-right corner of the palette to display the palette menu. Drag down to flatten the image. Alternatively, you can choose **Layer, Flatten Image**.

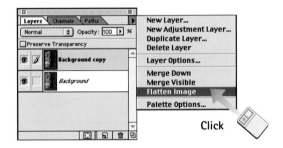

Click

2 Choose File, Save As

Regardless of the current format of the file, you change the file format from the **Save As** dialog box. Choose **File, Save As** to open the dialog box. Note that the **Save As** dialog box will not display even a flattened image if that image contains extra channel information.

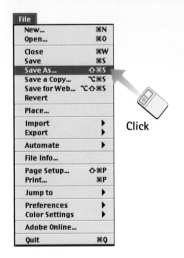

Click

3 To Save as JPEG

You save a file in JPEG format if you have a photographic image that must be compressed for onscreen viewing (such as the Web). From the **Save As** drop-down list box, select **JPEG**. In the **JPEG Options** dialog box that opens, move the **Quality** slider to control the degree of compression. You will lose detail at low settings, but better image quality (higher settings) increases file size.

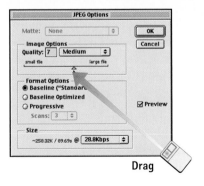

Drag

4 To Save as PDF

Choose the PDF format for Web documents that must keep layout and design consistent with print versions. To save a file in PDF format, choose **Photoshop PDF** from the **Save As** drop-down list box. In the **PDF Options** dialog box that appears, move the **Quality** slider to determine compression. It is also a good idea to enable the **Embed ICC Profiles** check box to control color shifts across multiple systems.

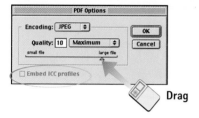

Drag

5 To Save as TIFF

You can save a file in TIFF format when you want to save a clipping path with the file to be used in a program such as Illustrator, PageMaker, or InDesign. To save a TIFF file, choose **TIFF** from the **Save As** drop-down list box. Click **OK** to open the **TIFF Options** dialog box. Specify whether the file must be compatible with a Mac or PC. In addition, you almost always should enable the **LZW Compression** check box, which dramatically compresses the file size without any impact on image quality.

End

How-To Hints

LZW Slows Things Down

Saving a TIFF file as LZW does have its drawbacks—mainly that opening and closing files takes longer because Photoshop has to compress and decompress the data. For smaller files, it's no big deal, but for files that are more than 10MB, you will notice the difference.

Be Careful Saving JPEGs

The image quality of a JPEG file will erode if you repeatedly save the file as JPEG. The compression doesn't just happen one time—it is reapplied with every save. You should convert the file to JPEG only at the very end, when the image editing is complete.

How to Optimize Color Files for Printing

Preparing a file for printing means a lot of different things. It could mean a complicated offset professional color project with film and plates, or it could refer to an inkjet proof or a laser print. For the sake of argument, this task refers to color printing on a press or proofing device. It is important that you check with your printer before prepping files and setting things up, because all printers do things a bit differently. What follows are general guidelines for how to optimize a file for printing.

Begin

1 Determine Output Resolution

In most cases, you will print at 300dpi for high-quality images. You can reduce this number slightly for some offset presses (inkjet and color printers and copiers are even more forgiving). Open the **Image Size** dialog box by choosing **Image, Image Size**. If you know the resolution requirements required by your printer, type them in the **Resolution** field; if you don't, type **300** as a baseline and select **pixels/inch.** Make sure that the **Resample Image** check box is not selected.

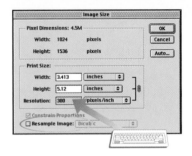

2 Set the Dot Gain

Dot gain helps compensate for the ways ink spreads and is absorbed on different kinds of paper. Ink spreads a lot more on newsprint, for example, which requires compensation to keep the dots from filling in completely. Choose **File, Color Settings, CMYK Setup** to open the **CMYK Setup** dialog box. Type the appropriate value in the **Dot Gain** field. For standard proofing printers, leave this at the default; check with your offset printer for specific compensation settings.

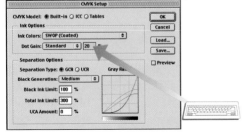

3 Set the Printing Target

Unless your printer specifies otherwise, if you're printing in color, set the **Ink Colors** field in the **CMYK Setup** dialog box to **SWOP (Coated)**; leave the other settings unchanged. The other settings apply primarily to offset printing and vary from press to press and shop to shop. Ask your printer for advice on how to handle these settings.

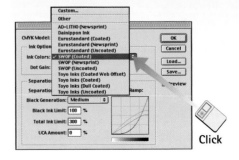

Click

4 Check for Out-of-Gamut Colors

To print in color, you have to convert the color mode for your image to CMYK. Because the CMYK color format allows fewer colors than, say, the RGB format, you could lose some of the colors in your image during the color conversion. Choose **View, Gamut Warning**. The gamut mask points out the areas where colors could be lost in the image so that you can address the problem before the image goes to the printer.

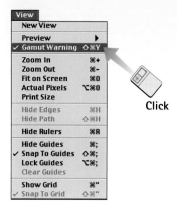

Click

5 Correct Problem Colors

After you identify where the problem colors lie, choose **View, Gamut Warning** again to turn off the gamut mask and then choose **View, Preview, CMYK**. Photoshop displays a preview of how the colors will look when they are converted. These color shifts are often subtle, and you may decide you can live with them. If not, edit colors using any of the color tools. (**Hint**: The **Sponge** tool may soften some saturated colors.)

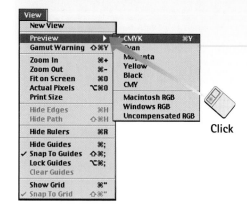

Click

6 Convert File to Proper Color Mode

After you correct any color problems, convert the file to CMYK format. Choose **Image, Mode, CMYK Color** to convert the file.

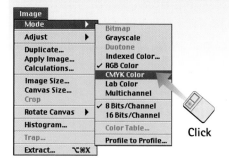

Click

7 Save File in Proper Format

Save the file in the proper format, as specified by your printer: Choose **File, Save As** and then select the desired format from the **Format** drop-down menu. If in doubt, save the image as an **EPS** file (for a PostScript device) or as a **TIFF** file (for a standard device).

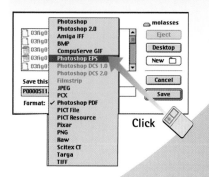

Click

How to Move Files from Mac to Windows

There's more to moving a file from a Mac machine to a Windows machine than handing off a file. The same image looks darker in Windows because most Mac monitors are calibrated at a gamma of 1.8; Windows monitors usually are calibrated at 2.2. Moving a file from Mac to Windows can lead to some very muddy results if the image is dark to start with on the Mac. When moving a file from Windows to Mac, the *gamma factor* is less of an issue because of the cross-platform capabilities built into the Macintosh. As long as the **PC Exchange** settings are correct, files should move over without a problem.

Begin

1 Open File in ImageReady

In Photoshop, open the file you want to move from the Mac to Windows (choose **File, Open** and select the file from the **Open** dialog box). With the file open in Photoshop, you can easily open it in ImageReady by choosing **File, Jump to, Adobe ImageReady 2.0** (or by clicking the **Jump to** button at the bottom of the toolbox).

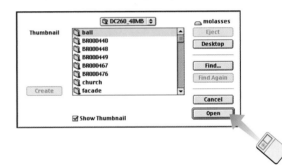

Click

2 Set Preview for Windows Gamma

If you're using a Mac, choose **View, Preview, Standard Windows Color.** If you're using Windows, choose **View, Preview, Standard Macintosh Color.** Observe the image on your screen. This option gives you an accurate preview of what the file will look like on the other platform.

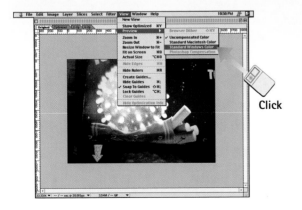

Click

3 Choose Adjust Gamma

Now adjust the image gamma: Choose **Image, Adjust, Gamma** to open the **Gamma** dialog box. Click the **Macintosh to Windows** button or the **Windows to Macintosh** button; the slider adjusts automatically. Drag the slider to make any further modifications. Toggle the **Preview** check box on and off to check the appearance of the image.

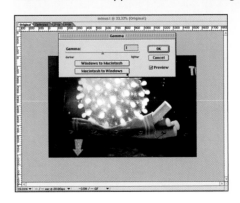

4 Save as Proper Format

From the **Optimize** palette, select the proper file format (either GIF or JPG). Then choose **File, Save Optimized** to save a copy of the file. If you're not sure which file format is best for the image, you can switch between the two and get an idea, in real time, which format will look better and take up less file space. To do so, simply toggle between the two options in the **Optimize** palette.

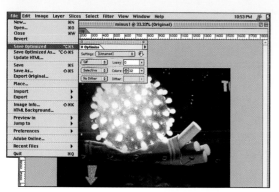

5 Use Windows-Compatible Disk

When sending the file from Mac to Windows, copy the file to a floppy disk that has been formatted in PC format. If you are sending the file electronically, be sure to zip the file to protect it during transmission.

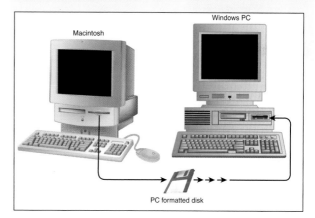

End

How-To Hints

Converting in Photoshop

Preparing files for use on another platform (Windows-to-Mac or Mac-to-Windows) works best in ImageReady, although you also can do it from Photoshop. Choose **View, Preview, Windows RGB** to preview how a Mac file will look in Windows. If you're on a Windows machine, you can preview how the Mac gamma will affect an image by choosing **View, Preview, Macintosh RGB**.

How to Build GIF Files for the Web

GIF files are efficient, compact files perfect for use on the Web. As you see in the tasks that follow, GIF files allow you to build in transparency and animation while keeping the file size small. GIF files do not handle photographic images well, however. If you want your photographic images to maintain detail, consider the JPEG file format.

Begin

1 Open and Save File in Photoshop

In Photoshop, choose **File, Open**. The **Open** dialog box appears. Select the file you want to convert to GIF format, and click **Open**. Choose **File, Save for Web**. The **Save for Web** dialog box opens, and Photoshop creates a duplicate image, leaving the original image untouched.

2 Select Optimized File Format

From the first drop-down menu, select **GIF**. Leave the next two options set at **Selective** and **Diffusion** (these options refer to the color conversion and dither patterns).

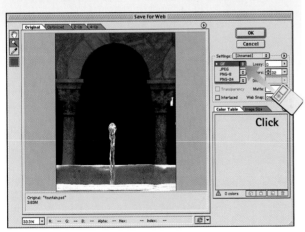

Click

3 Set Lossy and Dither Sliders

Set the **Lossy** and **Dither** sliders. Start by setting **Lossy** at **100** and **Dither** at **0**. To reduce the file size, keep the **Dither** value as low as possible and the **Lossy** value as high as possible. The image is updated to reflect the changes you make. Watch the image changes to help make a final decision when it comes to applying the various settings.

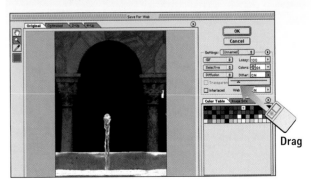

Drag

4 Preview Your Settings

Click the **Optimized** tab to preview the file compression results based on your settings. If the image is too grainy, lower the **Lossy** slider. If it appears solarized and graphic, raise the **Dither** value.

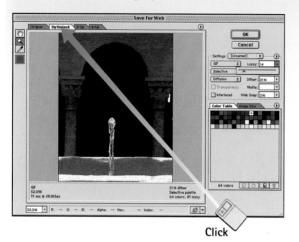

Click

5 Set the Number of Colors

Your next goal is to create a GIF file with as few colors as possible. Shoot for 32 or 64 (some graphics file can use as few as 8 or even 4 colors without compromising the image much). Click and hold the **Colors** drop-down list and select the number of colors. (Alternatively, highlight the number in this field and type the desired value.)

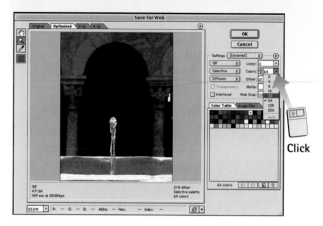

Click

6 Save the File

Click **OK** to close the **Save for Web** dialog box. The **Save Optimized As** dialog box opens. Verify the name and location of the file and click **Save** to save the file.

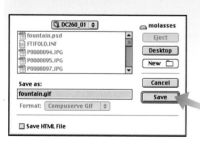

Click

End

How-To Hints

Use 2-Up or 4-Up Comparison Tables

If you're unclear about multiple compression settings, click the **2-Up** and **4-Up** tabs in the **Save for Web** dialog box. These tabs enable you to compare options side by side.

Jump to Original Mode Before Changing Multiple Sliders

When you are working with the **Optimize** slider, each change you make redraws the preview—which can slow things down considerably, especially when you want to adjust multiple variables. To speed things up, click the **Original** tab, change the settings, and click the **Optimized** tab again to view the changes to the image.

How to Optimize GIF Color Sets

The more you work with GIF conversion, the more you realize that the most critical step is in mapping the original colors to a minimal yet representative table set. To most people, it sounds inconceivable that 32 colors can replace the thousands of colors in an image. Although you *can* do it, you must be careful about which colors you keep and which you throw away.

Begin

1 Open and Save File in Photoshop

In Photoshop, choose **File, Open**. The **Open** dialog box appears. Select the file you want to convert to the GIF format and click **Open**. Choose **File, Save for Web**. The **Save for Web** dialog box opens, and Photoshop creates a duplicate image, leaving the original image untouched.

Click

2 Set Basic GIF Settings

Refer to Task 4 and set the compression type (**GIF**) and the **Dither** and **Lossy** settings. From the **Colors** list, select the lowest number of colors while keeping the file's integrity intact. Click the **Optimized** tab to review the results.

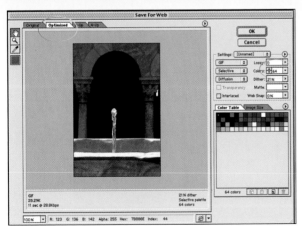

3 Lock Important Colors

Click the **Color Table** tab to bring it to the forefront. Click the **Eyedropper** tool in the **Save for Web** dialog box and click a prominent color in the image. The corresponding color in the color table is highlighted. Lock the selected color by clicking the **Lock** button at the bottom of the color table. Locking a color prevents it from being removed or dithered, which can be important for large areas of solid color. Repeat this step for any primary colors in the image.

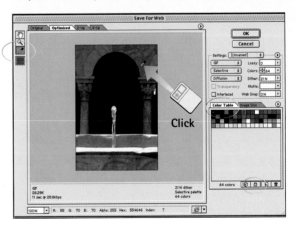

Click

4 Eliminate Close Colors

With this image showing on the **Optimized** tab, choose **Sort by Luminance** from the Color Table palette menu. In the **Color Table**, select a color close to a locked color and choose **Delete Color** from the Color Table palette menu. The screen redraws to delete the selected color from the image. Continue deleting colors until you get a core set that represents the image well.

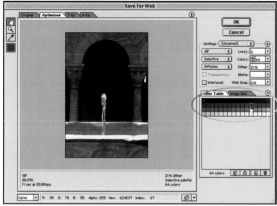

5 Changing Individual Table Colors

With the important colors locked down, determine whether you need to change other colors. To change color swatches, double click the color in the Color Table; the **Color Picker** dialog box opens. Change the current color, paying close attention to the Web-safe icon in the picker (the 3-sided box icon), which shows you the nearest Web-safe color.

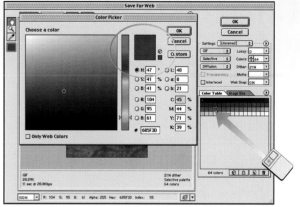

Double-click

6 Save the Color Table

If you're working with the same kind of image, or you want a series of images to use the same color set, save the Color Table you just fine-tuned. Choose **Save Color Table** from the Color Table palette menu. In the **Save As** dialog box that appears, type a name for the CLUT (Color LookUp Table) profile and click **OK**.

Click

End

How-To Hints

Using a Saved Color Table

To load a saved CLUT profile, open the **Save for Web** dialog box and choose **Load Color Table** from the Color Table palette menu.

Use Web-Safe Colors

Use the **Web Snap** slider in the top-right corner of the **Save for Web** dialog box to convert existing colors to Web-safe colors. Change the slider and monitor the results in the preview. The higher the value in the **Web Snap** slider, the more exactly colors are transformed to the Web-safe palette. The **Web-safe palette** refers to a subset of colors that can be reproduced exactly the same on all platforms and with all browsers. Use these colors to ensure that people who will see your Web graphics see exactly the colors you intended them to see.

How to Create a GIF Transparency

GIF files have an advantage over JPEG files in that they enable you to set certain areas as transparent. This means that you can create silhouette effects to place over Web page backgrounds. The transparent areas in a GIF file are completely invisible. In contrast, PNG files allow varying degrees of transparency. This task uses ImageReady to create the transparency. Although Photoshop has a wizard that creates a transparency, that wizard does not enable you to tweak the GIF optimization or preview the file.

Begin

1 Open File in ImageReady

In **ImageReady**, choose **File, Open**. In the **Open** dialog box, select the file you want to work with and click **Open**.

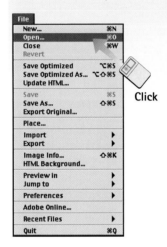

Click

2 Select the Area to Be Transparent

Using any of ImageReady's selection tools (such as the **Magic Wand** tool to select areas of similar color), make a selection representing the area you want to make transparent.

3 Apply a Layer Mask

Open the **Layers** palette by choosing **Window, Show Layers**. With the selection from Step 2 still active, press and hold the **Option/Alt** key and click the **Add Layer Mask** button at the bottom of the **Layers** palette. This action "masks out" the selected area, giving you an idea of what the final result will be.

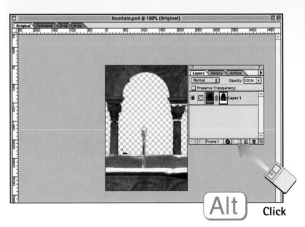

Alt Click

4 Build Optimize Settings

When the transparency is the way you want it, choose **Window, Show Optimize** to open the **Optimize** palette. Then specify the appropriate settings. (Refer to Task 4, "How to Build GIF Files for the Web," for instructions on setting up a GIF file.)

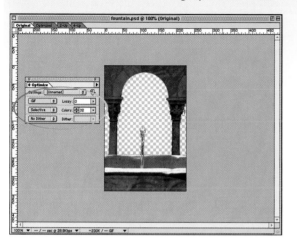

5 Preview in a Browser

Choose **File, Preview, <selected browser>** to look at the file as it will appear in a browser.

6 Save Optimized File

If the file looks good, close the browser and return to ImageReady. Choose **File, Save Optimized** to save the file using the settings in the **Optimize** palette.

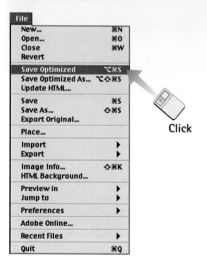

Click

How-To Hints

Fix the Transparency

If the transparency in the layer mask in Step 3 is not right, click the **Add Layer Mask** button in the **Layers** palette and paint the transparent selection as you would with any layer mask. (See Part 11, Task 6, "How to Add a Layer Mask," for complete details on layer masks.)

End

How to Build JPEG Files for the Web

The JPEG format works well for continuous-tone images, such as photographs. Even though the compression format creates artifacts that pixelate the image, these snags are hardly visible in photographic-quality images (although they can degrade the quality of hard-edged graphics). Photoshop 5.5 has a blur function built into the JPEG dialog box that is helpful for many images. You can smooth over many of the artifacts that surface when the quality level gets too low.

Begin

1 Open File in Photoshop

In **Photoshop**, choose **File, Open**. In the **Open** dialog box, select the file you want to compress with the JPEG format.

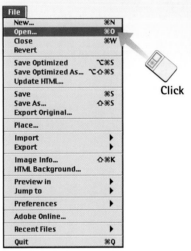

Click

2 Set JPEG Options

Choose **File, Save for Web** to open the **Save for Web** dialog box. From the **Optimized File Format** drop-down list, select **JPEG**. The main control in this section is the **Quality** slider. This setting determines the level of compression in the file, as well as the corresponding quality. Adjust the setting to high, medium, or low, remembering that the higher the quality, the bigger the file size; the lower the quality, the smaller the file size.

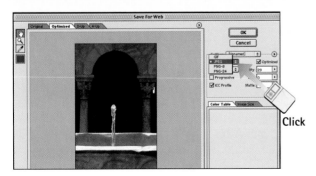

Click

3 Select 4-Up to Compare Settings

Click the **4-Up** tab to look at the original image and three variations. This comparison can help you select the setting that creates the highest-quality image combined with the lowest file size.

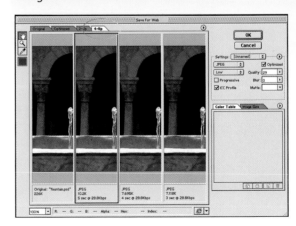

4 Tweak Blur Slider

Click the **Optimized** tab to return to that page and slightly raise the **Blur** slider to see whether this adjustment helps smooth the image. Click **OK** and rename the file to optimize it and save it as a separate file.

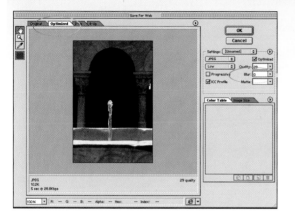

5 Reopen File

To check the quality of the image you just created, choose **File, Open**. From the **Open** dialog box, select the optimized file you just created. Check it again to make sure that the detail is solid and that the color is good. In this example, compare the quality of the original PSD file with the newly created JPG file.

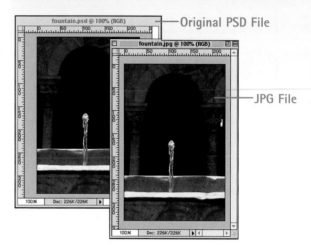

Original PSD File

JPG File

6 Test Unsharp Mask Filter

Because JPEG files tend to soften the original image, you may find that a slight **Unsharp Mask** filter helps bring back some detail (the filter also adds to the file size). Choose **Filter, Sharpen, Unsharp Mask**. Start by setting the **Amount** field to **50** or **100** percent; set the **Radius** field between **.7** and **1.0**. If you like the results, click **OK** to apply the mask; if not, click **Cancel**.

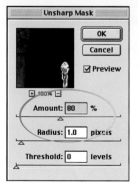

How-To Hints

Moving the Image Around

You can place the mouse cursor over the preview image in the Unsharp Mask dialog box ; when the pointer changes to the hand icon, move the image around so that you can look at specific details in the image.

End

How to Save a Transparent PNG File

PNG files aren't used very much because they are not compatible with some browsers. PNG files are based on an indexed color model. (All the Color Table features listed in Task 5 also apply to PNG files.) There are two types of PNG files: PNG-8 files use 8 bits of data and tend to be slightly smaller than comparable GIF files because they use a more efficient algorithm. PNG-24 files use 24 bits of data and are unique in their capability to support transparency and varying levels of opacity in a file. The downside to PNG-24 files is that they tend to be larger than their JPEG counterparts.

Begin

_1_ Open File in Photoshop

In **Photoshop**, choose **File, Open**. From the **Open** dialog box, select the file you want to compress with the PNG format.

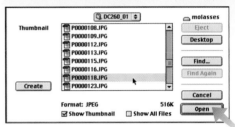

Click

_2_ Create Transparency

Select the **Eraser** tool from the toolbox. In the **Eraser Options** palette that opens, choose the **Airbrush** option. Erase the desired area in the image, modifying the transparency as necessary. Note that you are "painting" in some transparent areas on the image.

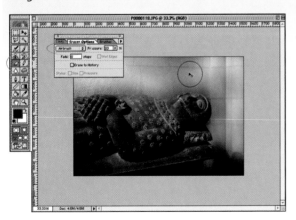

_3_ Choose Save for Web

After you finish creating the transparent areas, choose **File, Save for Web** to open the **Save for Web** dialog box.

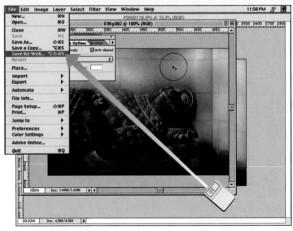

Click

4 Choose PNG-24 Format

Choose **PNG-24** from the **Optimized File Format** drop-down list and make sure that the **Transparency** check box is enabled.

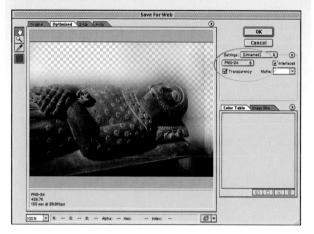

5 Apply a Matte

If the image is going up against a colored Web background, you can simulate the effect and check the dither by specifying a matte of the same color. To do this, disable the **Transparency** check box. Click and hold the **Matte** drop-down list and drag to select a color from the palette. (Alternatively, type a hexadecimal value in the **Matte** field.)

End

How-To Hints

The PNG Format and Today's Web Browsers

The PNG format holds great promise for things to come as far as Web graphics are concerned. Unfortunately, none of today's Web browsers uses the best features available with this file format. PNG files can have varying levels of transparency, for example, which no other file format has. Future browsers will undoubtedly offer support for these features, and we can only hope that support will come sooner rather than later.

Task

5

Working with Tone

*T*his part looks at how to work with image tonality. As far as digital images are concerned, *tonality* refers to the grayscale values from 0 to 255 that differentiate the image pixels. Tonality is black and white and shades of gray, tonality is a histogram, a halftone, salt and pepper, the *I Love Lucy* show, and a dark foreboding sky hanging low over the concrete streets of New York.

I'm using this somewhat poetic introduction to emphasize the fact that tonality is one of the most expressive elements of an image. It can establish a full-contrast range, create a feeling of darkness and danger, or obliterate outlines in the form of fog or mist. If you want to create a strong feeling in an image, consider exaggerating the tonality in some way.

In addition to its expressive qualities, tonality also helps to sharpen an image, even as it increases the contrast. Sharp details, rich and complex color, and the look of texture are all created by manipulating black, white, and shades of gray.

The tasks that follow will help you to optimize any given file, making it the best it can be. You can take a dark or underexposed image and make it usable with curves and a few filters. Even better, you can take an image that already looks pretty good and make it a real winner. ●

How to Measure and Compare Pixel Values

Knowing how to accurately measure pixel values is an important first step in being able to evaluate and correct digital images. Many times, you have to determine the tonal value of an image area or compare the value of two different areas. It is important to measure these values numerically, because pixel values change from monitor to monitor based on contrast settings, ambient light, and monitor brands. Photoshop uses the **Info** palette to measure pixel values; the **Eyedropper** and **Color Sampler** tools also are helpful aids.

Begin

1 Open the Info Palette

With the image open, choose **Window, Show Info**. The **Info** palette opens on the desktop.

Click

2 Select a Color Model

The top-left section of the **Info** palette represents the actual color value of the currently selected pixel. Click and hold the **Eyedropper** icon to select the color model in which you want the pixel's color specified. (Refer to Part 1, Task 6, "How to Select Colors," for information about color models.) Choose the **Opacity** option to measure the degree of transparency in a given layer.

Click

3 Select a Variable Color Model

The top-right section of the **Info** palette tracks a second set of color values, which allows you to compare the same pixel value with two different models. Click and hold the **Eyedropper** icon and select the desired color model from the list. Move the mouse cursor over the image (don't click) and watch the corresponding readings appear in the palette.

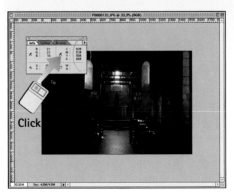

Click

4 Enter Coordinate Units

With so many pixels in an image, it can be hard to sample the same one more than once. The pixel coordinates section in the lower-left corner of the **Info** palette tracks the exact cursor position based on the x,y axis. Click and hold the cursor icon to choose the units of measure.

Click

5 Create Sample Points

To accurately track the same value through the course of your imaging session, you should use eyedropper sample points. Click the **Eyedropper** tool in the toolbox; a submenu of two eyedroppers appears. Select the **Color Sampler** tool (the second tool). Drag the tool over the image and click to place a sample point. A new section is created in the **Info** palette for each sample point you create.

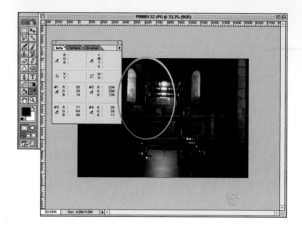

6 Track Sample Values

Drag the sample point to move it; drag the point off the image to delete it. Each image supports up to four sample points. If you want, you can set a color model for each point area in the palette, just as you did in Steps 2 and 3.

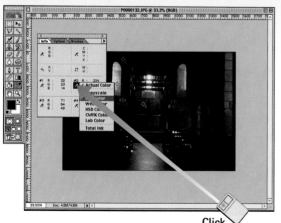

Click

How-To Hints

Selection Dimensions

Use the width/height section in the lower-right corner of the **Info** palette to measure the exact size of an active selection. This capability is especially valuable with the **Marquee** tool, which gives real-time dimensions as you drag. For more information on selections, see Part 3, "Selection Techniques."

End

How to Optimize the Tonal Range

When you capture an image with a digital camera or scanner, chances are that the tonal range in your image is lacking in highlights or shadows. An *optimized tonal range* is one in which the darks are completely black, the highlights are white, and the other tones are well distributed. In Photoshop, you adjust the tonal range of an image with the **Levels** option. Not only does adjusting tone ensure good contrast and detail, it can correct any unwanted color casts. Even if the image looks pretty good to start with, optimizing the tone can improve things even further.

Begin

1 Open the Info Palette

Open the image for which you want to adjust the tonality. Choose **Window, Show Info** to open the **Info** palette.

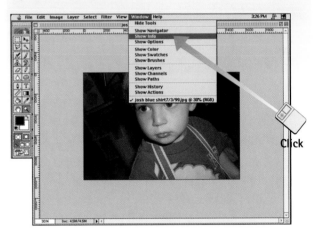

2 Open Levels

Choose **Image, Adjust, Levels** to open the **Levels** dialog box.

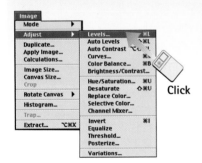

3 Select the Black Point

Click the black **Eyedropper** icon in the lower-right corner of the **Levels** dialog box. Move the cursor over the image; the pointer changes to an eyedropper as it enters the image. Using the readings from the **Info** palette, find the darkest area of the image and click to set the black point.

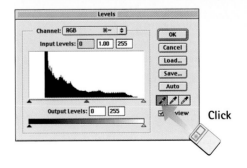

4 Select the White Point

Click the white **Eyedropper** icon in the lower-right corner of the **Levels** dialog box. Move the cursor over the image; the pointer changes to an eyedropper as it enters the image. This time, find the lightest area of the image and click to set the white point.

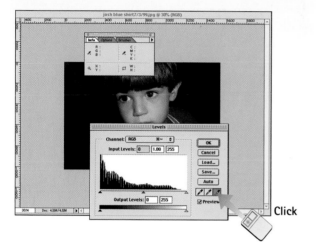

Click

5 Click OK

Click **OK** to apply the effect. By setting the black and white points for the image, you are telling Photoshop what the darkest shadows and brightest highlights in the image are. Doing so establishes the tonal range of the scanned image. You can experiment with setting a black point that is not the darkest area of the image or a white point that is not the brightest area of the image to see what effect this "skewed" tonal range has.

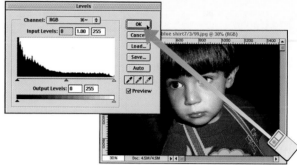

Click

End

How-To Hints

Reselect the Darkest or Lightest Area

Take your time when looking for the lightest and darkest points in the image. Selecting a pixel that is not close enough to the light or dark point can result in blowing out the highlights or shadows. If you make a mistake, press the **Option (Alt)** key and click the **Reset** button (the **Cancel** button changes to the **Reset** button) to make another attempt.

How to Improve Contrast with Curves

Task 2 showed how to use the **Levels** dialog box to set the white point and the black point of an image, thus optimizing the tonal range for the image. You can use the **Curves** dialog box to increase the contrast in the image, allowing you to selectively enhance image details. If the image seems flat or lacking in contrast, curves can make a dramatic improvement.

Begin

1 Open the Info Palette

Open the image you want to affect. Choose **Window, Show Info** to open the **Info** palette.

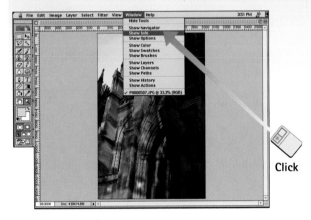

Click

2 Open the Curves Dialog Box

Choose **Image, Adjust, Curves** to open the **Curves** dialog box.

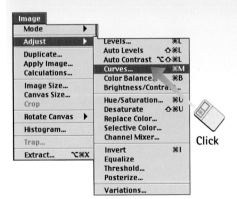

Click

3 Set the Black and White Points

Follow the steps in Task 2 to set the black and white points for the image. Use the **Eyedropper** icons from the **Curves** dialog box rather than those in the **Levels** dialog box.

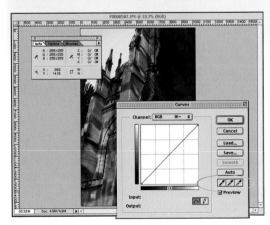

4 Darken Shadows

Click the lower-left portion of the diagonal line in the **Curves** dialog box to place a point on the curve. If necessary, slowly drag the point you placed downward to darken the shadow areas in the image.

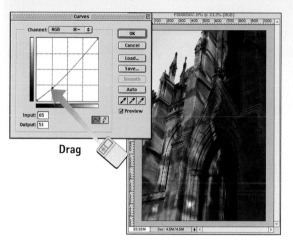

Drag

5 Brighten Highlights

Click the upper-right portion of the diagonal line in the **Curves** dialog box to place a point in the light areas. Slowly drag the point up to lighten the highlights, increasing the overall contrast, especially in the midtones. Click **OK** to apply the effect.

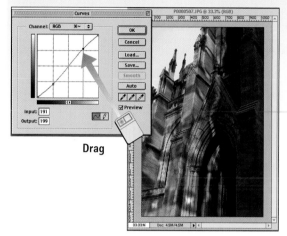

Drag

End

How-To Hints

Check the Input and Output Values

In the **Curves** dialog box, watch the **Input** and **Output** values to understand exactly what changes you're making to the curve. The **Input** value refers to the original pixel values (for example, a midtone value of 128). Clicking at an **Input** value of 128 and dragging up to 160 means that all pixels originally valued at 128 are now a lighter value of 160. In addition, all pixel values around the input value are lightened so that the effect is applied smoothly. Keep the curve shape smooth, and the effect will look natural.

How to Use the Dodge, Burn, and Sponge Tools

At times, you will want to lighten or darken an image only in select areas. Although you could select an area and make changes only to that area (see Part 3, "Selection Techniques"), you may find the **Dodge**, **Burn**, and **Sponge** tools more effective. These tools allow you to brush your corrections onto an image: The **Dodge** tool lightens the image, the **Burn** tool darkens it, and the **Sponge** tool lets you saturate or desaturate the color intensity.

Begin

1 Select the Proper Tool

Open the image you want to affect. Click and hold the **Dodge** tool in the toolbox. A pop-out menu appears, from which you can select the **Dodge**, **Burn**, or **Sponge** tool.

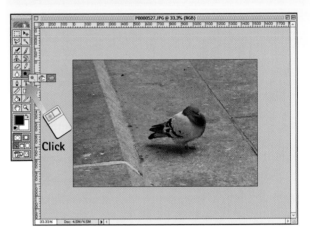

2 Set the Options Palette

Double-click the tool to open the **Options** palette for that tool (you also can choose **Window, Show Options**). Depending on the area of the image you want to modify, select **Highlights**, **Midtones**, or **Shadows** from the drop-down menu. For the **Sponge** tool, select **Saturate** or **Desaturate** to increase or decrease the color intensity.

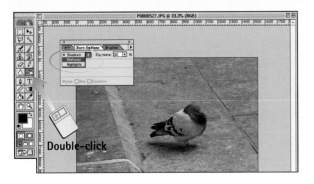

3 Set the Exposure

Exposure refers to the degree of effect applied to the image as you use the selected tool. You also can think of it as intensity or pressure. In the **Options** palette, click and drag to adjust the **Exposure** slider. Select a higher percentage number for a dramatic effect; select a lower number for subtle changes.

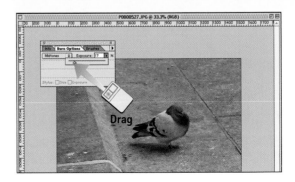

4 Select a Brush

Choose **Window, Show Brushes** to open the **Brushes** palette. Select a suitable brush size for the tool you're working with and the image you're editing. To avoid hard-edged brushstrokes, select a feathered brush.

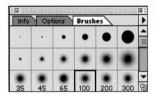

5 Begin Brushing in the Effect

Begin with a very low exposure and a feathered brush that is large enough to cover the desired area in just a few strokes. Repeatedly brush over the area, building up the effect as you go. If a pronounced brushstroke appears, undo the stroke (choose **Edit, Undo Burn Tool**) and lower the exposure. Click and drag lightly to apply the effect, instead of dragging back and forth.

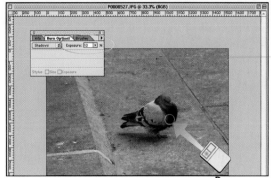

Drag

6 Change Brush Size and Exposure

As you work, select a smaller brush size as needed to work into smaller areas. If you change the brush size, consider decreasing the exposure to hide the brushstrokes. This may be necessary because smaller brushstrokes are more visible when repeatedly applied.

End

How-To Hints

To Undo the Effect

Because these effects are applied with repeated brushstrokes, choosing **Edit, Undo** does not revert the image to its appearance before you began. Give yourself a safety net by opening the **History** palette and creating a snapshot before you begin. (See Part 2, Task 4, "How to Undo with the History Palette," for more information.) After the effect is applied, click the snapshot to revert to the previous state or to compare the result.

Brushing in a Straight Line

To brush the effect along a straight line, click once at the start of the line, press and hold the **Shift** key, and click at the end of the line. Photoshop applies the effect in a straight line between the two points.

How to Sharpen Images

Sharpening images with Photoshop is a very common and useful task. If your image appears soft or blurry, you can bring back detail, clarity, and contrast with sharpening. Sharpening brings out additional detail in virtually all images except those created on the highest-quality scanners. The best way to add overall sharpness to an image is to use the **Unsharp Mask** filter. Be careful not to over-sharpen, which results in an unnatural halo around the objects in the image, flattening the space. If this occurs, choose **Edit, Undo** and reapply the effect.

Begin

1 Select the Unsharp Mask Filter

With the image open, choose **Filter, Sharpen, Unsharp Mask**. The **Unsharp Mask** dialog box opens.

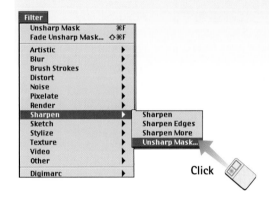

Click

2 Set the Amount Slider

Enable the **Preview** check box and set the thumbnail view to **100** by clicking the + or – button. The **Amount** slider controls the degree of sharpening applied to the image. Adjust the slider as needed, noting the changes in the preview window in the dialog box.

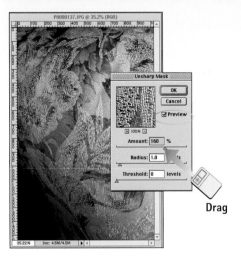

Drag

3 Set the Radius Slider

The **Radius** control determines whether the effect is applied to a single pixel or a group of pixels. A higher radius value lowers image detail in exchange for higher overall contrast. For the most naturalistic images, begin by setting this option at **1** and don't let it rise above **3**.

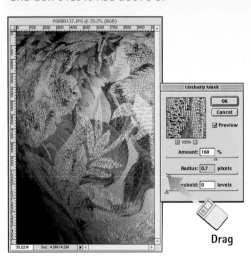

Drag

4 Set the Threshold Slider

The **Threshold** setting excludes a portion of the tonal range from receiving the effect. Leave it at **0** to apply the effect globally; move it higher to exclude tones from dark to light. For all practical purposes, you typically do not change this setting.

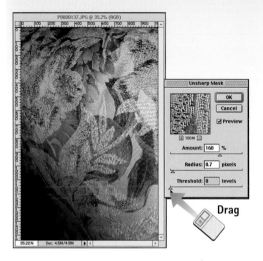

Drag

5 Apply the Effect

You can use the scrollbars in the image window to scroll to different areas in the image. Check the image carefully to ensure that all areas are sharpened to the proper level. When you are satisfied with the image, click **OK** to apply the effect.

Click

6 Fade the Result as Necessary

Choose **Filter, Fade Unsharp Mask**. After the **Fade** dialog box opens, move the **Opacity** slider to the left to gradually decrease the sharpen effect as necessary. If you decide to soften the effect, set the slider accordingly and click **OK**, leaving the **Mode** setting at **Normal**. If you determine that the initial effect is acceptable, click **Cancel** to close the dialog box and leave the image unchanged.

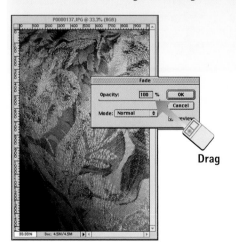

Drag

How-To Hints

Don't Forget About Color

Sharpening an image is as much about color as it is about tone. Be sure to color balance your images to maximize overall contrast and color vibrancy.

Unsharp Mask Does It All

Notice that Adobe lists other sharpening filters in the **Filters, Sharpen** submenu. These options are all rolled into the **Unsharp Mask** dialog box, which you can use to apply all the other filters. Don't waste your time with the other filter options—**Unsharp Mask** is all you need.

End

How to Use Blur to Sharpen

Although it may sound paradoxical, you actually can use the **Blur** filter to *sharpen* an image. Specifically, you can blur one area of your image to make the other area look sharper. In this task, you intentionally soften the background areas of an image, making the subject appear sharper in comparison. This is a good approach for images that are too soft to be remedied using the **Unsharp Mask** filter alone.

Begin

1 Open the File in Photoshop

Choose **File, Open** and select the desired file.

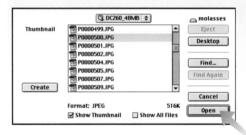

Click

2 Apply an Unsharp Mask

Begin by sharpening the image as much as you can. Choose **Filter, Sharpen, Unsharp Mask** and follow the directions in Task 5 to sharpen the image.

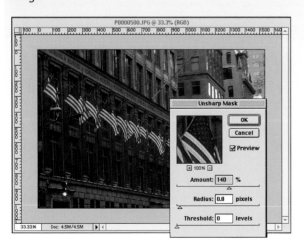

3 Select the Background

Using Photoshop's selection tools, select the area to which you want to apply the blur. For more on making selections in Photoshop, see Part 3, "Selection Techniques."

4 Feather the Selection

Feathering softens the edges of a selection, helping it to blend with unselected areas. Choose **Select, Feather**. In the **Feather Selection** dialog box, specify the desired pixel value. The amount of feathering you choose depends on the overall resolution of the image and the subject matter. Click **OK** to apply the effect.

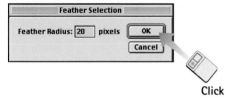

Click

5 Apply Gaussian Blur

Choose **Filter, Blur, Gaussian Blur** to open the **Gaussian Blur** dialog box. (Gauss was a mathematician; the Gaussian blur effect is based on his mathematical formulas.) Adjust the **Radius** slider until the proper blur amount appears in the window. Click **OK**.

6 Touch Up with the Blur Tool

After deselecting the selection (press ⌘+D or **Ctrl+D**), select the **Blur** tool from the toolbox and brush in the smaller areas to complete the blur transition.

How-To Hints

Don't Overdo It

The blur effect works best when it is subtle and subliminal. Resist the urge to knock the background way out of focus.

Build Up the Blur Effect

In the **Blur** tool palette, keep the **Pressure** setting relatively low so that you can build the effect with multiple brushstrokes. This will give you more control and accuracy.

End

How to Convert Images to Grayscale

If you are going to print a color image in black and white, it's a good idea to convert a copy of it to grayscale first. At first glance, converting an image to grayscale seems like an easy task: You choose **Image, Adjust, Desaturate** to remove all the color (or better yet, let the printer force the image to gray). What could be easier? The problem with this approach is that the proper tonal range for all image areas may not be emphasized. In this task, you optimize the tones so that there is detail everywhere, ensuring that the central subject is well represented.

Begin

1 Open the File in Photoshop

Choose **File, Open** to open the desired color image.

Click

2 Convert to Lab Color

Choose **Image, Mode, Lab Color** to convert the image to the Lab color space. Lab color maintains a better range of tones in the image than does any of the other color models.

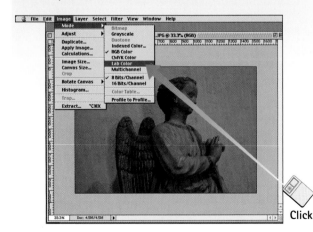

Click

3 Open Channels

Choose **Window, Show Channels** to open the **Channels** palette. Click the visibility icons (the eye icons) for the **a** and **b** channels to turn them off. Only the **Lightness** channel should be visible.

4 Modify with Curves

Choose **Image, Adjust Curves** to open the **Curves** dialog box. Modify the curves as described in Task 3 to enhance the contrast and range for your image as necessary.

5 Duplicate Channel

With the **Lightness** channel still selected, open the **Channels** palette menu and choose **Duplicate Channel**. In the dialog box that appears, name the new file and choose **New** from the **Destination** pop-up menu. This action saves the **Lightness** channel to a new file, which you can modify further.

Click

6 Close the Original File

Close the original file by choosing **File, Close**. Select **Don't Save** in the dialog box that appears to leave the original file untouched.

End

Task

6

Working with Color

*F*or some people, color corrections are very intimidating. They see the RGB or CMYK conversion curves and tables, talk to prepress guys who harp over perfect flesh-tone balance, and decide that color correction is something to be left to the "experts."

Although it's true that you can mess up the color in an image, it's also true that you can do quite a bit on your own. This is especially the case if you're designing for the Web as opposed to print: The monitor is much more representative of the way the final image will look on the Web as opposed to its appearance on paper.

The tasks in this part explain the basics of color correction and show what a huge difference color can make in an image. Although you won't be a prepress expert, you should learn to trust your eye a bit more and to have confidence in correcting the color in your own images.

For the tasks in this part, it is very important that you've run the monitor calibration wizards described in Part 1, "Getting Started with Photoshop." If you have not done so already, run the Gamma Wizard and the Color Management Wizard before you continue with the tasks in this part. ●

How to Work with Color Variations

If you're not familiar with color correction and color theory, variations is the place to start. The **Variations** dialog box is an intuitive color-correction tool that lets you correct color visually instead of using sliders, curves, and numbers. The dialog box features thumbnails of your image, with visual previews of how various color and tone corrections will look. The thumbnails are arranged to follow the standard color wheel, with primary colors opposite each other. As you work in this mode, notice how adding one color subtracts from the opposite color. For example, adding red subtracts from cyan.

Begin

1 Open the Variations Dialog Box

With the image file you want to affect open, choose **Image, Adjust, Variations** to launch the **Variations** dialog box. In the top left of the box are two images; they help you compare your original image and the current variation you have created. At the beginning, these images are identical, but they will deviate from each other as you work.

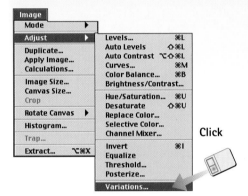

Click

2 Select a Tonal Area

Although all the controls in the **Variations** dialog box modify the entire image to some extent, the controls allow you to focus on one area of the tonal range at a time. Click the **Highlights, Midtones, Shadows,** or **Saturation** radio button to focus the correction on this one area.

Click

3 Modify the Color

Click any of the thumbnail images in the color wheel array of thumbnails to add the corresponding color to the original image. As you do, notice that the original image takes on the selected color cast; all the surrounding thumbnails reorient themselves to the new current image. As you continue clicking thumbnails, the color corrections continue to be applied in an additive way.

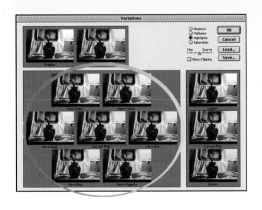

4 Modify the Coarseness Slider

As you get closer to the desired color, you may find that the variations between color choices are too broad. You may want to add a red that's somewhere between the current shade of the image and the **More Red** thumbnail. To create more subtle color shifts, move the **Coarseness** slider toward the **Fine** end of the scale. This adjustment makes all the color variations more subtle, allowing you to select the variation that looks the best.

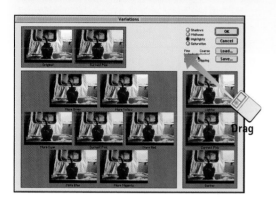

5 Modify the Tone

The three thumbnails on the right of the dialog box control the overall tone of the image. Click the top thumbnail to lighten the image; click the dark thumbnail to darken the image.

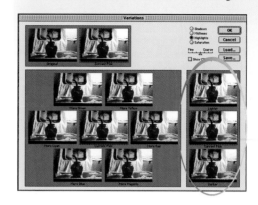

6 Save Settings

If you are working with a group of similar images, you may want to save your settings so that you can reload them at a later time with one mouse click. Click the **Save** button. After the **Save** dialog box opens, type a name for the settings file you are creating.

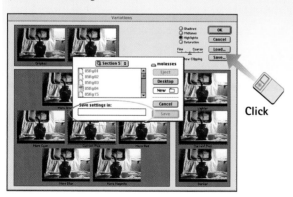

7 Apply the Color Correction

To reload the saved settings, open the image, open the **Variations** dialog box, click the **Load** button, and select the desired settings file. Click **OK** to apply the correction to the image.

End

How-To Hints

Check the Clipping

If you enable the **Show Clipping** check box in the **Variations** dialog box, Photoshop applies a mask to areas of the image that will not convert to CMYK. This mask lets you monitor whether your corrections will work for print.

How to Make Global Color Corrections

Global color corrections can fix an image that appears to have a color cast or overall tint. This color cast could have been caused by an input device (such as a scanner or digital camera) or by a light source (such as fluorescent lighting). This task shows you how to correct the tint of an image so that the image appears natural to the eye. You can apply this technique to images of natural subjects (such as trees and sky) as well as to more abstract projects.

Begin

1 Open the File

Choose **File, Open** and select the image file you want to edit.

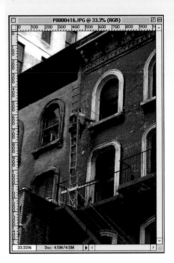

2 Open the Info Palette

Choose **Window, Show Info** to display the **Info** palette.

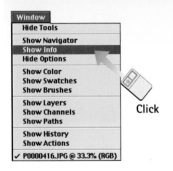

Click

3 Set the Black and White Points

If you haven't done so already, set the black point and white point, as explained in Part 5, Task 3, "How to Improve Contrast with Curves." In brief, open the **Curves** dialog box by selecting **Image, Adjust, Curves** and use the black point and white point eyedroppers in the **Curves** dialog box to set the points. Click **OK** to apply the effect.

4 Measure Values

Look at the image onscreen and search for areas that appear to have a color cast. A cast is especially evident in parts of the image that you know are supposed to be white or gray. With the **Curves** dialog box still open, move your mouse pointer over these areas and measure the results in the **Info** palette.

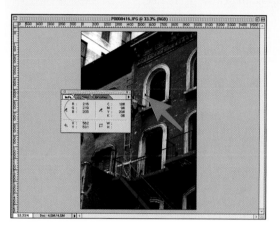

5 Evaluate the Results

In comparing the numbers, look for a number that is much higher or lower than the other two. In this example, the red and green are close in value, but the blue is low, indicating that the sample area is a bit yellow (the inverse of blue). If a number is low, its inverse is dominant; you must add to the low color to balance the color cast. (Red's inverse is cyan, green's inverse is magenta, and blue's inverse is yellow.)

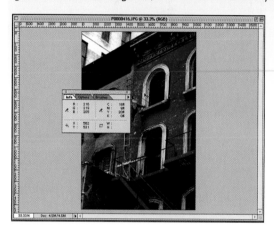

6 Open the Curves Dialog Box

This step corrects a specific color channel based on the evaluations made in the previous step. Click the arrow next to the **Channel** box and select the color you want to modify, based on your readings in Step 4. This action launches a curve that corresponds to that color channel only.

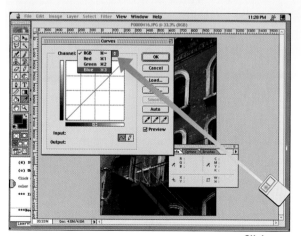

Click

7 Modify the Color

Click and drag the curve up or down, adding or subtracting the target color to eliminate the color cast from the image. Click **OK** to apply the change.

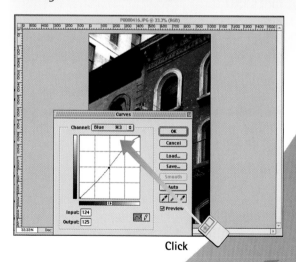

Click

End

How to Correct a Range of Colors

At times, you may want to change a range of colors within an object or area. You may want to make a red ball yellow, for example, or a blue car green. This involves changing more than just one color shade, because numerous values represent the highlights and shadows across the form. At the same time, you don't want to change any areas outside the desired object. Photoshop offers the perfect set of tools for making these kinds of changes: the **Select Color Range** and the **Hue Saturation** controls. This task shows you how to specify a range of colors and globally change them to another color.

Begin

1 Open the File

Choose **File, Open** and select the image file you want to modify.

Click

2 Select Color Range

Choose **Select, Color Range** to launch the **Color Range** dialog box. From the **Select** drop-down list box, choose **Sampled Colors** so that you can select the colors in the image that you want to change. In addition, select **White Matte** from the **Selection Preview** pop-up menu to preview the colors selected against a white background within the main image window.

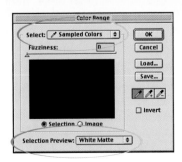

3 Sample the Color Range

The **Eyedropper** icon should be selected by default. If it's not, click it in the dialog box and then click in the thumbnail or main image to choose a color. The selected color is shown in the main image window against a white background so that you can see exactly what is included in the sampling. Drag the **Fuzziness** slider to increase or decrease the range of colors selected. Click **OK** to create a selection of the color range as shown.

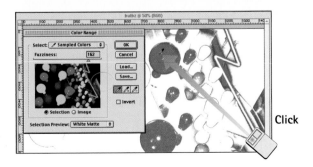

Click

4 Change the Hue

Choose **Image, Adjust, Hue/Saturation** to launch the **Hue/Saturation** dialog box. Drag the **Hue** slider to shift the color range as desired.

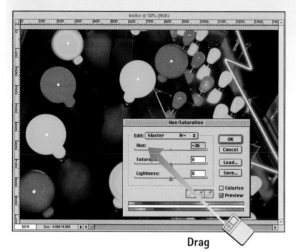

Drag

5 Check the Brightness

If the color range selected is very dark or very light, you may find that moving the **Hue** slider does not change anything. In this case, drag the **Lightness** slider and then modify the **Hue** slider as needed to achieve the desired effect.

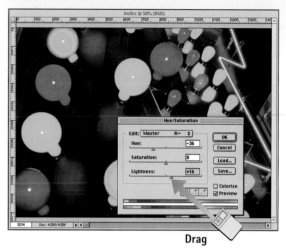

Drag

End

How-To Hints

Use the Photoshop Controls

Although ImageReady offers a **Hue/Saturation** dialog box, use the Photoshop version if possible. Photoshop's Hue/Saturation controls offer a more interactive interface, showing you what things will look like *as you move* the slider instead of forcing you to click **OK** before you can see the results.

Check Colorize

If you want the selected area to change to all one hue, enable the **Colorize** check box in the Hue/Saturation dialog box. This option lets you select a single hue for the selected range by moving just the **Hue** slider.

Select a Target Area First

As you specify a color range, it is normal for stray pixels from other areas such as the background to creep in and add "noise" to the image. To keep stray pixels to a minimum, select the object with any of Photoshop's selection tools before you sample a color range (see Part 3, "Selection Techniques"). You also can use the **Image, Adjust, Color Range** command to apply this same kind of effect.

How to Make Subtle Color Changes

All of Photoshop's color tools let you make subtle tweaks to the image, but the **Color Balance** command offers more control than the other tools—especially if you're changing the image globally. This approach lets you gradually shift the colors, isolating changes in the **Highlight**, **Midtone**, or **Shadow** areas. The effect is similar to adding a warming filter to a camera lens: Colors are enhanced rather than completely changed.

Begin

1 Open the File

Choose **File, Open** and launch the image file you want to modify.

Click

2 Select Color Balance

Choose **Image, Adjust, Color Balance** to launch the **Color Balance** dialog box. Enable the **Preview** check box to make sure that the changes are updated in the main window as changes are made.

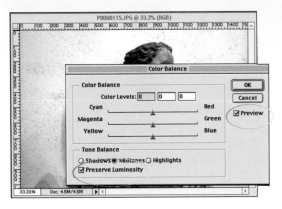

3 Target a Tonal Range

Target the primary tonal area to be modified. Should the color shift be applied primarily to the shadows, midtones, or highlights? In this example, you'll start with the midtones and work into the shadows. Select the corresponding option to target that specific area.

Click

4 Shift the Color

Move one of the three color sliders toward the color you want to add to the selected tonal range. In this example, drag the **Cyan/Red** slider toward **Red** and notice the changes in the midtones of the angel image.

Drag

5 Check Other Tonal Ranges

Click the two remaining tonal range buttons and add color in those areas as well. This step is necessary especially if you want to apply a color correction globally across the entire range of the image. When finished, click **OK** to apply the effect.

End

How-To Hints

Change the Range to Which You Are Applying Color

The **Color Balance** tool isolates the color changes in specific areas in the tonal range (shadows, midtones, or highlights). If a given correction is not having the desired effect, switch tonal ranges.

How to Build Duotones for the Web

Duotones are grayscale images that are tinted for a graphic effect. Although they originally were designed to push the tonal range of standard grayscale images, designers have embraced duotones for their graphic look and feel. This task shows you how to set up a pseudo-duotone effect for the Web, adding a second color to tint a grayscale image. Task 6 addresses setting up actual duotone plates for print.

Begin

1 Open the File

Choose **File, Open** and launch the image file you want to modify.

2 Convert to Black and White

If you are starting with a color image, choose **Image, Adjust, Desaturate** to convert the file to a black-and-white monotone image. The **Desaturate** command eliminates the colors in the image but maintains the preexisting color channels. The **Desaturate** option is what allows us to add color again in subsequent steps.

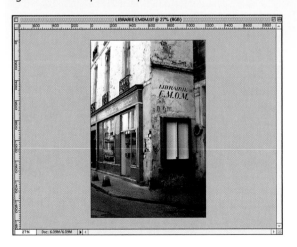

3 Optimize Tonal Range

Set the white point and black point as explained in Part 5, Task 2, "How to Optimize the Tonal Range." Select **Image, Adjust, Curves** to open the **Curves** dialog box; select the black or white eyedropper to set a black or white point and optimize the tonal range. Now you have an optimized black-and-white monotone image to work from.

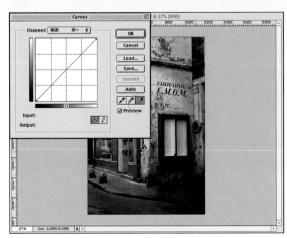

4 Select Hue/Saturation

Choose Image, Adjust, Hue/Saturation to open the Hue/Saturation dialog box. Make sure that both the Preview and Colorize check boxes are enabled.

5 Select the Color

The Colorize option adds an initial red cast to the entire image. Adjust the Hue slider to select a different color.

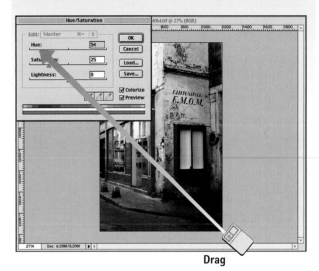

Drag

6 Modify the Lightness

If your image is predominantly dark, you may have to adjust the Lightness slider to push color into the shadow areas. When you're done adjusting the colors for the image, click OK to close the dialog box and apply the effect.

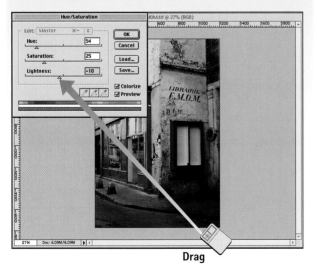

Drag

How-To Hints

Keep the Saturation Low

A true duotone effect has subtle colors that are tempered by the addition of the black plate. For a true duotone effect, resist the temptation to increase the saturation to more than 30.

End

How to Build Duotones, Tritones, and Quadtones for Print

Where a duotone adds one color to the black plate, a *tritone* adds two colors to the black plate, and a *quadtone* adds three colors to the black plate (for totals of three and four colors, respectively). Work closely with your printer to create a plan for setting percentages and proofing the image before printing. This task shows you how to apply the settings and set up the file for the printer; your printer representative should help you define the settings.

Begin

1 Open the File

Choose **File, Open** and launch the image file you want to modify.

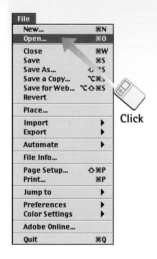

Click

2 Convert to Grayscale

If you started with a color image, choose **Image, Mode, Grayscale** to convert the color model from its original color set to a true grayscale image.

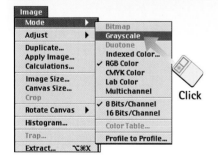

Click

3 Optimize the Tonal Range

Set the white point and black point as explained in Part 5, Task 2, "How to Optimize the Tonal Range." Select **Image, Adjust, Curves** and select the black or white eyedropper from the **Curves** dialog box to set the black or white point and optimize the tonal range. Now you have an optimized black-and-white monotone image to work from.

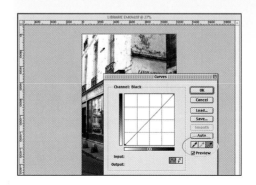

4 Open the Duotones Dialog Box

Choose Image, Mode, Duotone to open the Duotone Options dialog box. This dialog box does not open unless you are using a grayscale image. Click the Type pop-up menu and select Duotone.

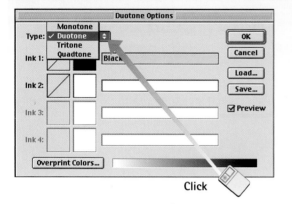

Click

5 Apply the Color

Click the blank color swatch below the black color swatch to launch the Custom Colors dialog box, which defaults to the Pantone Coated standard. (You can select a different color set from the list if you want.) Click a swatch to see it applied to your image. Click OK to return to the Duotone Options dialog box. (You can also select a color other than black. To do this, click the black color swatch and choose a color.)

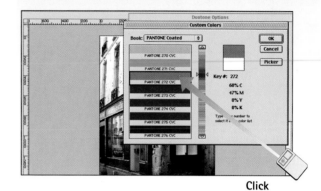

Click

6 Set the Tonal Curve

The *tonal curve* determines which areas in the image are affected by the second color. Click the Curve button next to the Ink 2 label to launch the Duotone Curve dialog box. Click the diagonal line in the curve grid and drag it up or down to add or subtract the color in that area. The image updates as you do this, so trust your eyes more than the numbers unless you are following required specs from your printer. Remember that you can also change the curve for the black plate, represented by the Ink 1 label. To do this, click the Curve button and make changes as necessary.

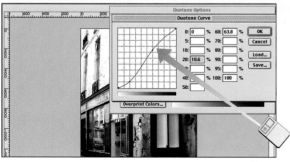

Drag

7 Add Additional Colors

If you select Tritone or Quadtone from the Type box in the Duotone Options dialog box, Photoshop creates one or two additional ink sets. Select colors and set the curves as described in Steps 5 and 6 for each of the ink sets. Click OK to apply the effect.

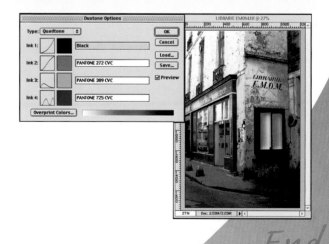

End

Task

7

Image Editing Basics

*T*his part of the book looks at the basic skills you need to modify and process most kinds of images. It is inevitable that you will need to resize, rotate, flip, or silhouette almost every image you work with. These basic tasks are important because you must know how to do them before you can apply more advanced processing. In addition, if you do not perform tasks such as silhouetting and resizing properly, you may destroy image resolution or create unprofessional results.

These tasks sometimes are referred to as *preprocessing tasks* or even *image prep tasks,* implying that they are a precursor or requisite step before more serious work can begin. A better way to look at the process is to consider these tasks as fundamental skills that every Photoshop user must master. Exercising these skills with speed and precision will bring a high level of consistency and quality to all of your work.

An area you should pay special attention to is resizing images safely to minimize loss of image quality. Images are made up of small building blocks called *pixels*; the number of pixels in an image's width and height determines the image's resolution. Consider an image that is 500 pixels high and 700 pixels wide. If you ask Photoshop to increase the image size to 700 high by 900 wide, you are asking it to add pixels. Where do these pixels come from? Photoshop makes them up, using a process called *interpolation*.

When adding a new pixel, Photoshop looks at the surrounding pixels to determine the value of the pixel it will add. When Photoshop interpolates an image, it can use one of three methods: Bicubic, Bilinear, and Nearest Neighbor. With the Bicubic method, Photoshop looks at the pixels on all four sides as well as on all diagonals and makes a guess at what the new value should be. With the Bilinear method, Photoshop looks only at pixels vertically and horizontally. With Nearest Neighbor, Photoshop looks only from side to side to make the decision of what the new pixel should be.

As you can imagine, the Bicubic method delivers the highest level of quality for most photographic images—although it takes the longest to process. And although the Nearest Neighbor method generally provides the lowest quality for photos, it does a great job on hard-edge, graphic shapes and is also the fastest method of interpolation. ●

How to Resize Images

The size of a Photoshop image is measured in width and height, combined with a resolution value expressed as *pixels*, or *dots per inch (dpi)*. For example, you could have a 4×5–inch image at 300dpi. When resizing images, it is important to understand your minimum target resolution and to never go below it. (For example, in the print world, 300dpi is generally a target resolution.)

Begin

1 Open the Image in Photoshop

Choose **File, Open** and select the image file you want to work with.

Click

2 Check the Image Size

Choose **Image, Image Size** to open the **Image Size** dialog box. Make sure that the **Constrain Proportions** check box is enabled. This option ensures that the width-to-height ratios are maintained and prevents you from distorting the image as you resize it.

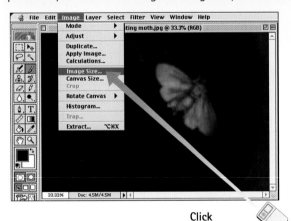

Click

3 Deselect Resample Image

Make sure that the **Resample Image** check box is disabled. Deselecting this option keeps you from accidentally degrading image quality, especially if you plan to enlarge the image.

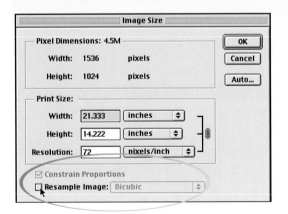

4 Enter Target Resolution

Resolution refers to the number of dots per inch (dpi) or pixels per inch (ppi). For print, you want the image resolution to be between 225dpi and 300dpi; in contrast, the Web needs only 72ppi. Type the target resolution for this image in the **Resolution** field. As you do this, the dimensions (the **Height** and **Width** fields in the **Print Size** area) should change, ensuring that image quality is not sacrificed. In this case, typing **300** in the **Resolution** field changed the dimensions from 14×21 to approximately 3×5.

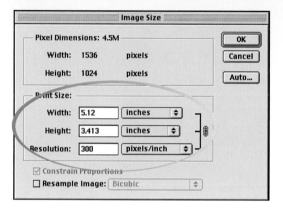

5 Enter Target Dimensions

Because resolution is tied to image dimension, changing the dimension values modifies the target resolution you entered in Step 4. To change dimensions without altering resolution, enable the **Resample Image** check box and select **Bicubic** as the interpolation method. If you are designing for the Web, enter the dimension size in the fields in the **Pixel Dimensions** area; if you are designing for print, use the **Print Size** section. Specify the units of measurement in the pop-up menus (remember that image quality degrades if you enable the **Resample Image** check box), and then increase the image dimensions. Enter the desired dimensions and click **OK** to resize the image.

End

How-To Hints

Resizing Graphics

When resizing graphics with hard edges and flat color, you may get better results by choosing **Nearest Neighbor** from the **Resample Image** pop-up menu rather than **Bicubic**. Nearest Neighbor creates very crisp lines and hard edges, preserving more of the original look of the design.

Enlarging Size and Reducing Resolution

You should avoid enlarging image dimensions without decreasing resolution. For example, to enlarge a 4×5 image at 600dpi to 5×7, you should reduce the resolution to approximately 425dpi. This precaution keeps you from interpolating the image and losing detail. If you deactivate the **Resample Image** check box in the **Resize Image** dialog box, Photoshop automatically makes these adjustments for you.

TASK 2

How to Add Canvas

Task 1 looked at how to scale an image up or down by increasing the resolution or dimensions of the image itself. In contrast, this task explains how to keep the image the same size and just add more workspace around it. Photoshop calls this extra workspace *canvas* and enables you to specify exactly how much is added. Adding canvas is important when adding and combining images, adding flat color for text, or any time you need to increase the image dimensions without enlarging the image data.

Begin

1 Open the Image

Choose **File, Open** and select the image file you want to work with.

2 Set the Background Color

When you add canvas to an image, the canvas is filled automatically with the current background color. Click the **Background** color swatch in the toolbox. The **Color Picker** dialog box opens; use this dialog box to select a color for the background of the canvas you will add. Or, you can move the cursor into the image area to sample a color from the image itself. Alternatively, you can leave the background set to white.

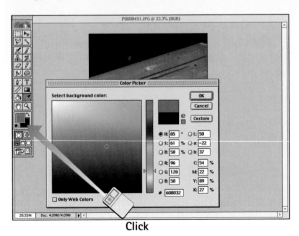
Click

3 Open the Canvas Size Dialog Box

Choose **Image, Canvas Size** to open the **Canvas Size** dialog box.

Click

132 PART 7: IMAGE EDITING BASICS

4 Specify Anchor Placement

The **Anchor** diagram lets you specify where the extra canvas is added. The darkened box represents the current image; the remaining grid represents the canvas to be added. Click in the diagram to move the dark box and control where the extra canvas is placed.

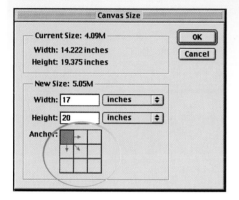

5 Specify Dimensions

Note the current size of the image at the top of the dialog box. Type values for the new image size in the **Width** and **Height** fields in the **New Size** area. Use the drop-down menus to specify units of measurement, if necessary. Click **OK** to apply the effect. This example shows the canvas added when I moved the **Anchor** box to the upper-left corner of the grid and increased the width of the image from 14.222 inches to 17 inches and the height of the image from 19.375 inches to 20 inches. Notice that the extra space appears as blank canvas around the original image.

End

How-To Hints

Transparent Background

When an image has no background layer, adding canvas always places transparent canvas rather than canvas that has the background color. To force the added canvas to have a white background, choose **Flatten Image** from the **Layers** palette menu. You also can fill the canvas to force the added canvas to white, or fill it by using the **Paint Bucket** tool, as explained in Part 8, Task 7, "How to Fill with the Paint Bucket."

How to Crop an Image

Cropping an image involves cutting an image down to a specific square or rectangular section, excluding all other unwanted areas. You may want to crop an image to fit it to a specific dimension or to enhance the composition. Sometimes cropping involves trimming away a little detail around the edges. At other times, you may isolate a small component of an image, discarding everything else. Cropping an image does not change the resolution or image quality; it only shrinks the canvas size as unwanted areas are eliminated.

Begin

1 Open the Image

Choose **File, Open** and select the desired image file.

2 Select the Crop Tool

Click and hold the **Marquee** tool in the toolbox and select the **Crop** tool from the pop-out menu that appears.

Click

3 Define the Crop Area

Click and drag the **Crop** tool over the image to specify the area to be cropped. A dotted line appears, showing what has been selected. If the selection is wrong, click outside the crop selection to deselect it, and drag again to specify the area. Everything outside the dotted rectangular area will not appear in the finished image area.

Drag

4 Modify the Crop Area

Notice that the crop area has handles at the corners and on the sides. To modify the crop area by extending a side, drag a side handle. To extend the crop area from two adjoining sides, drag a corner handle. To move the entire crop area, click inside the selected crop area and drag the box to a new position.

Drag

5 Rotate the Crop Area

You can even rotate the crop area. To do this, position the cursor outside of a corner handle until it changes to a rotate icon. Click and drag to rotate the crop box.

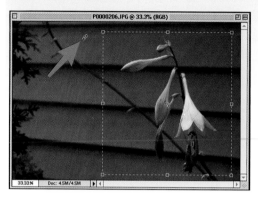

6 Crop the Image

When the crop selection is where you want it, double-click in the selection to crop the image. The image window is resized to display the new image with some blank canvas around it. The additional canvas represents the amount needed to "square off" the canvas area.

How-To Hints

Setting Crop Dimensions

To set a crop of a specific size, double-click the **Crop** tool to open the **Options** palette. Enable the **Fixed Target Size** check box and enter the dimensions in the corresponding spaces, leaving the **Resolution** field blank. With these settings activated, the **Crop** tool is restricted to the proportions in the **Width** and **Height** fields. You can enter a desired resolution if you want, although you should try to specify a resolution lower than what is currently used in the image.

End

How to Flip and Rotate an Image

You may have to reverse the orientation of an image for compositional or aesthetic reasons. This is relatively simple to do in Photoshop (provided that there is no text that would be reversed). In addition to reversing an image, you may want to rotate the entire image canvas, reorienting it to a new position. This is a common requirement for optimizing scans that were set up in the wrong direction. This process is similar to the **Free Transform** command discussed in Part 11, Task 3, "How to Transform Layers." The main difference is that **Free Transform** operates on individual layers rather than the entire image.

Begin

1 Open the File

Choose **File, Open** and select the desired image file.

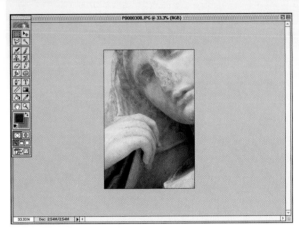

2 Rotate the Image

Select **Image, Rotate Canvas**. From the submenu, choose **90° CW** (clockwise), **90° CCW** (counterclockwise), or **180°**. In this example, I choose 90 degrees CW. The command is executed as soon as you select it from the menu.

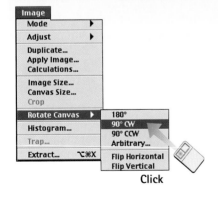

Click

3 Apply Arbitrary Rotation

Choose **Image, Rotate Image, Arbitrary** to open the **Rotate Canvas** dialog box. You can use this dialog box to specify the precise degree and direction of rotation. In this example, I want to rotate the image an additional **19** degrees clockwise (**CW**). Click **OK** to rotate the canvas, which enlarges to accommodate the angled image.

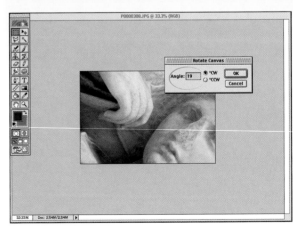

4 Flip the Image Horizontally

Choose **Image, Rotate Image, Flip Horizontal** to flip the image horizontally.

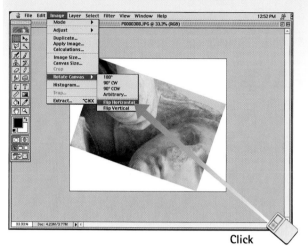

Click

5 Flip the Image Vertically

Choose **Image, Rotate Image, Flip Vertical** to flip the image vertically.

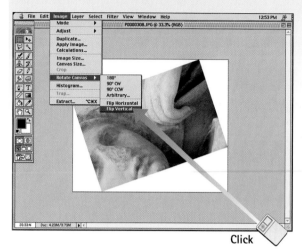

Click

6 Observe the Results

As you can see, rotating and flipping an image can greatly affect how the image is perceived. Although you haven't really changed anything about the image other than the way it is presented to the viewer, you can see that presentation is important.

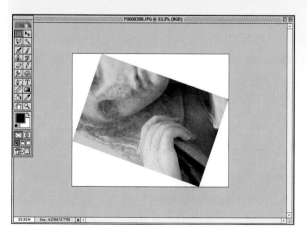

End

How to Silhouette an Image

Silhouetting an image refers to isolating part of an image against a white background, cutting it out from the rest of the frame. This task uses the **Extract** command to silhouette an image cleanly and easily. The **Extract** command asks you to define the edge of the object and then cuts it away from the background. Then you can smooth and modify the silhouette edges endlessly before you accept the final result.

Begin

1 Open the File

Choose **File, Open** and open the desired image file. Then choose **Image, Extract** to open the **Extract** dialog box.

2 Select the Edge Highlighter Tool

Select the **Edge Highlighter** tool from the minitoolbox in the upper-left corner. In the **Tool Options** area, drag the **Brush Size** slider to set an appropriate brush size. (Use a smaller brush size to define sharper edges more accurately; use a larger brush to highlight wispy, intricate edges such as hair or trees.) Then select highlight and fill colors from the pop-up menus, choosing colors that give a clear view of both the mask and the underlying image.

Click

3 Define a Silhouette Edge

Leave the **Smooth** setting at **0** and drag along the edge between the object and the part of the image to be erased. Be sure that the line overlaps both the object and the background. Don't be concerned with other object areas that touch the edge of the image you're tracing around.

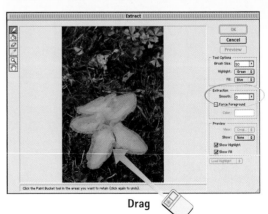

Drag

4 Fill the Object

Select the **Paint Bucket** tool and click in the outlined image area to fill the object.

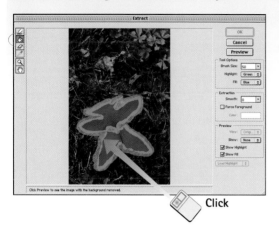

Click

5 Preview the Result

Click the **Preview** button to process a preview of the silhouette. Use the **View** drop-down list to switch between previews of the **Original** and **Extracted** images.

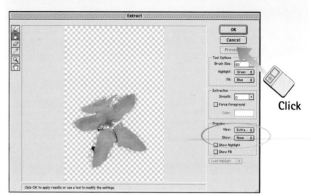

Click

6 Modify the Preview

If artifacts appear in the background, increase the **Smooth** slider to remove them. (In this example, notice that the dark bit of grass at the bottom -left edge of the leaf is minimized as the **Smooth** slider is adjusted.) You also can use the **Eraser** and **Paint Bucket** tools in the **Extract** dialog box to adjust the outline and fill as necessary. When the preview is accurate, click **OK** to extract the image.

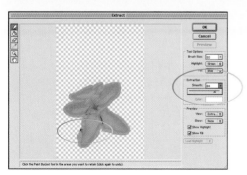

End

How-To Hints

Forcing the Foreground

If a single, flat color dominates the object, sample it with the **Eyedropper** tool from the **Extract** dialog box and enable the **Force Foreground** check box in the **Extraction** section of the **Extract** dialog box. This action selects all pixels matching the selected foreground color.

Other Methods

Although the new **Background Eraser** and **Magic Eraser** tools do similar things as the **Extract** command (see Part 8, Task 3, "How to Erase a Background"), the **Extract** command is especially suited for problem areas, such as smoke and fine-hair details.

Task

Drawing, Painting, and Filling with Color

*C*onsidering that Photoshop is often called a "paint" program, it's surprising how seldom the paint tools are used. Typical users will resize images, color correct, or apply a filter, but few people focus on the drawing or painting functions of the program.

Handled properly, the drawing and painting tools can yield predictable and acceptable results—even if your drawing skills are limited. Touching up images, spotting photographs, and erasing an area of a photo all involve the drawing and painting techniques described in the tasks in this part.

The underlying skill for almost all these tasks is the ability to effectively use a brush to apply the effects. When using a brush, the basic rule of thumb is to move from big and light strokes to small and heavy strokes. This means that you should start with the largest possible feathered brush set to the lightest possible setting. As you build up the effect, reduce the size of the brush to concentrate the results and slightly increase the pressure by increasing the **Opacity** slider. The one instance when this rule does not hold true is when you are doing line drawings and you want to put down a clean brushstroke.

The tasks in this part also look at filling areas with color or gradients. Although "filling" is certainly not the same as "brushing in" an effect, it does create a graphic effect that many people associate with digital drawing. ●

How to Paint an Image

Painting an image in Photoshop involves selecting a brush and applying an effect to an image. This task outlines the basic procedure for working with any of Photoshop's painting tools, regardless of the effect you are applying or the kind of file you're applying it to. Photoshop makes available these painting tools: **Airbrush, Paintbrush, Rubber Stamp, History/Art History Brush, Eraser, Pencil/Line, Sharpen/Blur,** and the **Dodge/Burn/Sponge** tools.

Begin

1 Select the Brush Tool

Open an image file. Click the **Paintbrush** tool in the Photoshop toolbox.

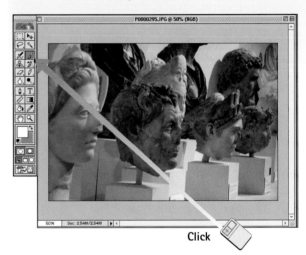

Click

2 Open the Options Palette

Choose **Window, Show Options** to open the **Options** palette for the current brush tool. Alternatively, you can double-click the brush tool to open the **Options** palette.

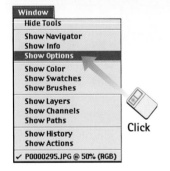

Click

3 Set the Opacity

The **Opacity** slider controls the density of the brushstrokes applied by the tool. Click and drag the slider to a lower setting for more transparent effects; leave it at 100 percent to paint with a completely opaque stroke.

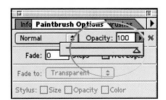

4 Choose a Brush

Choose **Window, Show Brushes** to open the **Brushes** palette. If the **Brushes** palette is grouped with the **Options** palette, you can just click the **Brushes** tab to bring it to the front. Click in the palette to select the desired brush size and feathering effect.

5 Paint the Image

To apply the paint effect, move the cursor into the image window and click and drag.

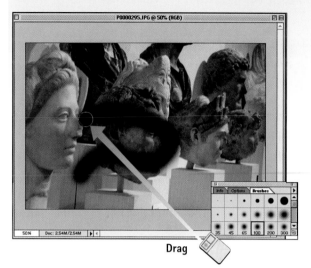

Drag

End

How-To Hints

Group Similar Palettes Together

You can group similar palettes together by clicking and dragging the palette tab and moving one palette onto another. Group the **Brushes**, **Options**, and **Info** palettes together because these often are used in tandem.

Tap in Big Brushes

To modify a large area without leaving telltale brushstrokes, use a large brush with a light **Opacity** setting. Instead of dragging, position the brush over the area and lightly click the mouse. Click repeatedly while moving the mouse slightly to build up a gradual effect.

Set Brush Size Preferences

You can set the Paintbrush cursor so that it appears as the currently selected brush size rather than as a tool icon or a set of crosshairs. This way, you know exactly how large the brush is (its circle icon shows you) in relation to the resolution of the image; you have a better sense of where you will paint the effect. Choose **File, Preferences, Display & Cursors** and click the **Brush Size** button from the **Painting Cursors** section of the dialog box.

How to Erase an Image

Erasing an image is the opposite of painting in the sense that it removes the current pixel values in the image window, based on the brushstrokes. When you erase, consider which Eraser tool you should use and what you want to erase. The **Eraser Options** palette offers four Eraser tool options: **Airbrush**, **Paintbrush**, **Block**, and **Pencil**. Use **Airbrush** to erase with a feathered brushstroke. The **Paintbrush** eraser is similar to the **Airbrush**, although it is not as soft. The **Block** eraser offers a flat, geometric effect that's perfect for hard-edged erasures, and the **Pencil** eraser lets you erase a single pixel at a time.

Begin

1 Select the Erase Tool

With the image you want to modify open onscreen, double-click the **Eraser** tool in the toolbox to select the eraser and pen in the **Eraser Options** palette. If the **Background Eraser** or **Magic Eraser** tool is selected, click and hold that tool and drag to select the **Eraser** tool from the pop-out menu that appears.

Background Eraser
Eraser | Magic Eraser

2 Choose an Eraser Type

Click the arrow to the right of the first drop-down menu in the **Eraser Options** palette and select the desired eraser type. Your options are **Paintbrush**, **Airbrush**, **Pencil**, and **Block**.

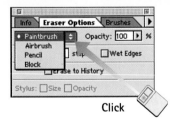

Click

3 Set the Pressure If Necessary

For all brush types except **Block**, click and drag the **Opacity** slider to set the desired opacity of the erasure effect. A lower value creates transparency; a high value erases the image more completely. If you want to soften an image rather than erase it, set a low value and brush over it several times.

Drag

4 Choose a Brush Size

If necessary, choose **Window, Show Brushes** to launch the **Brushes** palette. If the **Brushes** palette is grouped with the **Options** palette, click the **Brushes** tab to bring it to the front. For all eraser types except **Block**, select the desired brush size from the palette. When using the **Block** eraser, select the **Magnify** tool and click to zoom in (press the **Option** key—Windows users press **Alt**—and click to zoom out); this action creates the desired brush size relative to the image.

5 Erase the Image

Move the cursor into the image window and click and drag to erase the image. If you're using the **Block** eraser, you can click once to erase a clean square corresponding to the **Block** eraser size.

Drag

End

| 35 | 45 | 65 | 100 | 200 | 300 |

How-To Hints

Zoom for the Block Eraser

Although you cannot select smaller brush sizes for the **Block** eraser, you can click the **Magnify** tool in the toolbox and zoom in to erase tight areas.

Erase to History

Check the **Erase to History** check box in the **Eraser Options** palette to erase the image back to the **History** palette state, as specified by the **History Brush** selection setting. See Task 4, "How to Use the History Brush," for more information on using the **History** brush.

How to Erase a Background

Photoshop offers two ways to erase a background: the **Background Eraser** and the **Magic Eraser**. This task looks at how to use both tools, highlighting the differences between them. The **Background Eraser** erases an image area selectively, based on a pixel's value. It remembers the first pixel value you click on and then erases only that value, ignoring other values. This initial value is referred to as a *sample point* because the value of the pixel is used as a sample to determine how the eraser interacts with the image. You use the **Tolerance** slider to determine whether the brush erases the exact value sampled or a range of values based on the sample.

Begin

1 Select Background Eraser

With the image you want to modify open onscreen, select the **Background Eraser** from the toolbox. If necessary, click and hold the active **Eraser** tool and drag to select the **Background Eraser** from the pop-out menu that appears.

Click

2 Open the Options Palette

Choose **Window, Show Options** (or double-click the **Background Eraser** tool) to open the **Background Eraser Options** palette.

Click

3 Select the Eraser Type

Click the arrow to the right of the first drop-down menu in the **Options** palette and select **Find Edges**. This option erases adjacent pixels while maintaining strong edges—the perfect choice for eliminating the area behind the statue's head. The **Contiguous** and **Discontiguous** options do not keep as crisp an edge as **Find Edges** and do not work as well for this image.

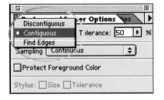

4 Estimate the Tolerance Setting

Always start with a low tolerance value and increase as you erase to keep a crisp edge to the image. The higher the **Tolerance** setting, the more the tool erases. Therefore, if there is high contrast between the background and object, set the **Tolerance** slider to a higher setting. The result will be a fast and clean erasure with a crisp edge. If the background and object are similar in contrast, use a low **Tolerance** setting and erase the area several times, perhaps using a smaller brush. Each image is unique; you'll have to experiment to find the right settings. To set the tolerance, drag the **Tolerance** slider in the **Options** palette.

Drag

5 Set the Sampling Option

Click the arrow next to the **Sampling** drop-down list and select **Once**, **Continuous**, or **Background Swatch**. The **Once** option samples only the pixels read when you first click the eraser on the image. As you continue to drag the eraser, only the initial pixel value is erased. The **Continuous** option samples continuously, allowing you to erase adjacent background areas of different colors. You can cover a wider range of pixels—although you run the risk of erasing the image edge. The **Background Swatch** option erases only the active color in the background swatch. With this option, you can select a background color, and the eraser erases only that specific color.

Click

6 Erase the Background

Move the cursor into the image window and click and drag to erase the background. Remember that the eraser looks at the pixel value where you click and erases only that value for as long as you drag the mouse. When you release the mouse and click again, you select a new sample point, and a new value is erased.

Drag

Continues

At this point, let's start over with the same image and use the **Magic Eraser** instead of the **Background Eraser** to get the job done. The **Magic Eraser** eliminates broad areas of the background with a single mouse click, in much the same way that the **Magic Wand** tool selects broad areas. When you click in the image, the **Magic Eraser** measures the pixel value you clicked and erases all adjoining pixels as well. For example, if you have a large flat area of solid color, a single click erases the entire area.

In these next steps, you use the **Tolerance** slider in the **Options** palette to specify how wide or narrow your erasure range will be. Increase the **Tolerance** setting to erase the full area in spite of slight variations in pixel values. Decrease the **Tolerance** setting to erase a more narrow range of pixel values. It helps to examine the image carefully and click the "best" spot to select the color you want to erase.

7 Select the Magic Eraser

Select the **Magic Eraser** from the toolbox. If necessary, click and hold the active **Eraser** tool and select the **Magic Eraser** from the pop-out menu that appears.

Click

8 Open the Options Palette

Choose **Window, Show Options** (or double-click the **Magic Eraser** tool) to open the **Magic Eraser Options** palette. Enable the **Anti-aliased** check box to create a smooth erasure edge. Enable the **Use All Layers** check box to erase across all visible layers. Enable the **Contiguous** check box to erase all adjoining pixels; leave it unchecked to erase the pixel value wherever it appears in the image.

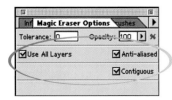

9 Erase the Image

Click in the image window to erase a range of pixels. If you don't like the result, choose **Edit, Undo**, revise the **Tolerance** setting, and try again. Continue clicking to delete the desired area.

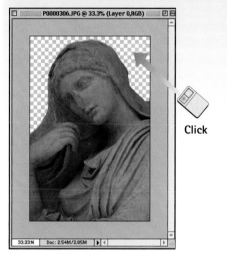

P0000306.JPG @ 33.3% (Layer 0,RGB)

33.33%　Doc: 2.54M/2.85M

Click

End

How-To Hints

Switching Tools

To switch quickly among the **Eraser**, **Magic Eraser**, and **Background Eraser** tools, press **Shift+E**.

Adjust Tolerance Often

Keep an eye on the areas you are erasing, and adjust the **Tolerance** setting up or down to optimize the amount of background being erased. Using a low tolerance setting may require you to sample often, erasing the background a chunk at a time. This may be necessary to keep a clean line of separation between the subject and background.

Preserve the Foreground Color

When using the **Background Eraser**, select the **Eyedropper** tool from the toolbox and sample the primary color of the foreground object. Then enable the **Preserve Foreground** check box in the **Background Eraser Options** palette to preserve the current foreground color as you use the eraser.

How to Use the History Brush

The **History Brush** allows you to selectively paint an iteration of an image from a previous state, as displayed in the **History** palette. Recall that as you work on an image, previous image states are recorded in the **History** palette. The **History Brush** lets you access these previous states as a source file, brushing them back into an image. The **History** palette stores only a limited number of states (as specified with the **History Options** command in the History palette menu). As you add states to the palette, you can convert a state to a snapshot to preserve that state. The basic rules of working with the **History** palette are outlined in Part 2, Task 4, "How to Undo with the History Palette."

Begin

1 Select the History Brush Tool

With the image file you want to modify open onscreen, select the **History Brush** tool from the toolbox. Note that all history states are erased when a file is closed; for this task, make sure that you are working with a file that has been modified from its original state since it was opened.

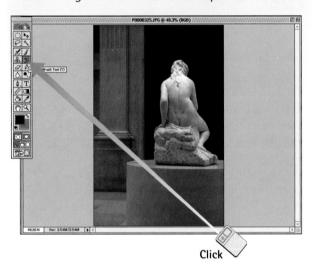

Click

2 Set the Options Palette

Choose **Window, Show Options** (or double-click the **History Brush** tool) to open the **History Brush Options** palette. Set the **Opacity** slider to determine the transparency or opacity of the brushstroke. For example, set the **Opacity** slider to 100 to add the history state as a solid area. Lower the **Opacity** slider to increase the transparency of the brushstroke.

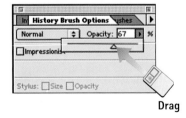

Drag

3 Select a Brush

Open the **Brushes** palette by choosing **Window, Show Brushes**. Select a brush size and a feathered effect from the palette.

4 Set the Source

Choose **Window, Show History** to open the **History** palette. Compare the various available history states and snapshots, and click the left column to place the source icon next to the state or snapshot you want to use as a source.

Click

5 Paint the Image

Move the cursor into the image window and click and drag to paint in the source image as it exists in the state you selected in the **History** palette in Step 4.

Drag

6 Look at the Results

In this example, the overall image was lightened and desaturated; then the shadows were painted back in from the previous history state to achieve the final results. The before and after images are shown here side by side so that you can see the differences.

End

How-To Hints

Painting in Corrections

The **History Brush** is a great tool for brushing color corrections into an image. Apply any of Photoshop's color-correction commands and then select the previous state from the **History** palette, undoing the effect. While still in the **History** palette, click in the left column next to one of the color-correction commands to set the **History Brush** source icon, as described in Step 4 (even though the tile is grayed out, you still can set the icon). Select the **History Brush** and brush the correction into the exact areas you want within the image.

How to Use the Rubber Stamp

The **Rubber Stamp** tool also is called the **Cloning** tool because it "clones" one area of an image, enabling you to paint it into another area. It can be useful for filling in an open area with a pattern or a color or for duplicating or repeating an object. The basic process for using the **Rubber Stamp** tool requires you to set a *source point* (the point from which the pixel values come) in the image and then to paint that value into another area of the image.

Begin

1 Select the Rubber Stamp Tool

Open the image file you want to modify. Double-click the **Rubber Stamp** tool in the toolbox to select the tool and launch the **Options** palette.

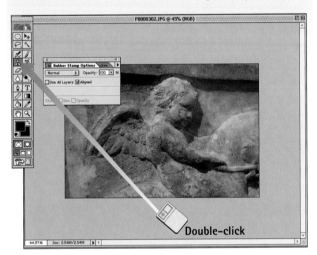

Double-click

2 Set Opacity

In the **Options** palette, click and drag the **Opacity** slider to set the transparency of the effect. For example, if you want to select a part of the image and apply it to another area on the image at the same intensity as the original, set the **Opacity** slider to **100**. Set the slider to **50** if you want the copied area to appear more transparent (lighter) than the original area.

Drag

3 Set the Aligned Option

Enable the **Aligned** check box if you want the reference point to move when you move the brush. For example, if you place the reference point to the left and down 50 pixels, the reference point will always be to the left and down 50 pixels as you paint with the brush. Leave this option disabled if you want the reference point to sample the same area every time you click the brush (the size of the area depends on the brush size you select).

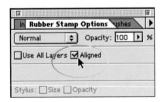

4 Select a Brush

Choose **Window, Show Brushes** to launch the **Brushes** palette. Select a brush size appropriate for the image. For the angel image example, you want to clone the entire face. A medium-sized brush with a slight feathered edge is your best choice for copying the face while blending it into the background.

5 Set the Reference Point

Move the brush into the image window and position it at the desired reference point. Press and hold the **Option** key (the **Alt** key in Windows) and click to set the reference point. The reference point is the starting point for the area you will clone. (Select a large brush size and click the eye, for example, to clone just the eye area of the angel's face.)

6 Stamp the Image

With the reference point set, click and drag in a new location (away from the original area) in the image. Notice that a crosshair (the reference point) effectively paints a copy of the original area in the new location. If the **Aligned** check box was not enabled, the specific area you referenced in Step 5 is the starting point, regardless of where you click.

How-To Hints

Sample All Layers

Enable the **Use All Layers** check box on the **Rubber Stamp Options** palette if you want the Rubber Stamp to sample all the layers as it paints. This is a good way to selectively consolidate material from multiple layers into one layer.

End

How to Build a Custom Brush

A painter in a studio has many brushes, each of which puts paint down a little differently, creating a wide range of painting effects. The same analogy hold true for Photoshop, which enables you to use many different brushes, each of which paints with a different kind of mark. The primary brush variables are size, softness, and angle. Photoshop has many standard brush shapes and sizes, but you can create a custom brush for a particular need. You may need a brush that is set at a specific angle to paint into a tight area, for example, or one that lets you cover an area with one click. Some custom brushes will correspond to a particular image, while others will be useful across a wide range of images.

Begin

1 Open the Brushes Menu

Choose **Window, Show Brushes** to open the **Brushes** palette.

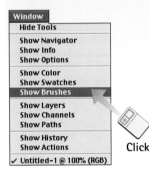

Click

2 Select New Brush

From the **Brushes** palette menu, choose **New Brush**. The **New Brush** dialog box opens.

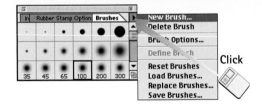

Click

3 Set the Diameter

Drag the first slider to set the diameter of the brush you are creating. You can specify a size ranging from 1 to 999 pixels. Watch the preview area in the lower-right corner of the dialog box as you set options for your new brush. The preview area shows brushes to size—up to 72 pixels. Beyond 73 pixels, it shows the brush to scale (as shown by the ratio numbers that appear above the box).

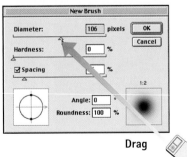

Drag

4 Set the Hardness

The **Hardness** slider determines whether the brush has a hard edge or a soft, diffused, feathered edge. Keep the slider at a low value for a soft effect; raise it for a more defined brush edge.

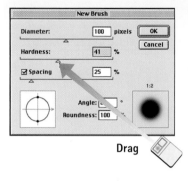

Drag

5 Set the Spacing

The **Spacing** option determines whether the brush paints in a smooth line or whether it makes a staggered series of marks, like a dotted line. Set the **Spacing** slider below **50** for a smooth line; raise it for a dashed effect. If you deselect the **Spacing Controls** check box, the spacing is applied at 100 percent, which creates a dashed effect if the brush is applied with a faster stroke.

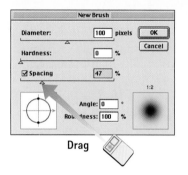

Drag

6 Set the Roundness and Angle

To brush an effect into certain areas, it can be helpful to have a brush that is not perfectly round. To build an elliptical brush, click and drag either of the black dots in the brush size diagram to create an oval. Then click and drag the horizontal axis line to change the angle of the oval. Click **OK** to add the brush to the **Brushes** palette, where it will be available for any other image you modify.

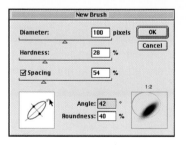

How-To Hints

Editing Existing Brushes

Double-click a brush in the **Brushes** palette to open the **Brush Options** dialog box. You then can change the parameters for that brush to alter the effect that brush has when you use it on an image.

Type in Brush Values

If you prefer, you can type the values for the settings in the **New Brush** and **Brush Options** dialog boxes instead of dragging the sliders and interactive controls.

End

How to Fill with the Paint Bucket

The **Paint Bucket** tool follows the same basic principle as the **Magic Eraser** you used in Task 3. The difference is that instead of erasing continuous pixels, the **Paint Bucket** tool changes the pixels to a single color. As with the **Magic Eraser**, you apply the **Paint Bucket** effect with a single mouse click. The **Tolerance** setting plays a big role in the final result.

Begin

1 Select the Foreground Color

With the image file you want to modify open, click the **Foreground** color swatch in the toolbox to select the fill color you want to use with the **Paint Bucket**. Select a foreground color from the **Color Picker** dialog box that appears. (With the **Color Picker** open, you also can select the foreground color by clicking in the image window itself.) In this example, I wanted to fill the dark left side of the image with red, so I chose a red foreground color. Click **OK** to close the dialog box and set the color.

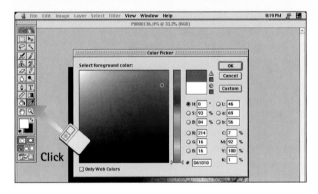

Click

2 Select the Paint Bucket Tool

Double-click the **Paint Bucket** tool in the toolbox to select the tool and open the **Paint Bucket Options** palette.

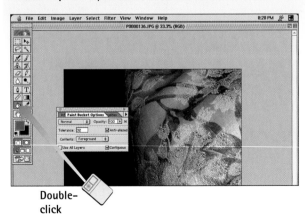

Double-
click

3 Set the Options Palette

Set the **Opacity** slider as desired to modify the transparency of the effect. Set the opacity to less than 100 to fill the area with a transparent fill. You will always set the **Contents** pop-up menu to **Foreground** unless you want to fill with a saved pattern. If no pattern is saved, the **Pattern** option will be grayed out. For details on saving patterns, see the next task.

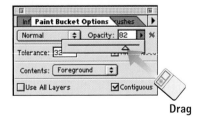

Drag

4 Set Tolerance

The **Tolerance** option determines how adjoining pixels are affected by the **Paint Bucket** tool. Type a high value in the **Tolerance** box to spread the effect across a wider tonal range. Type a low value to effect a narrow color set.

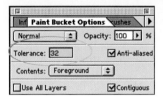

5 Fill the Area

Click in the image window to fill an area with the specified color. By default, the effect is confined to an area on a single layer, based on the **Tolerance** setting. You can target the entire image by enabling the **Use All Layers** check box in the **Paint Bucket Options** palette.

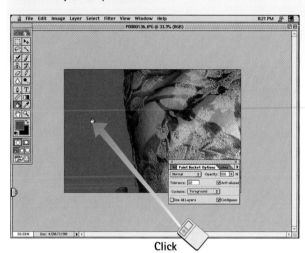

Click

6 Undo If Necessary

If the effect is too broad or narrow, undo it by choosing **Edit, Undo Paint Bucket** or by using the **History** palette. Alternatively, adjust the **Tolerance** setting in the **Paint Bucket Options** palette and reapply the effect.

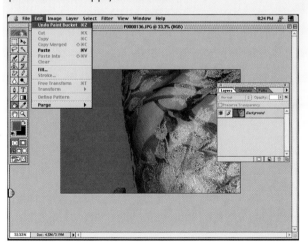

End

How-To Hints

Change All Values

By default, the **Paint Bucket** tool applies its effect to adjoining pixels of similar color. You can change *all* pixels of a similar value by deselecting the **Contiguous** check box in the **Paint Bucket Options** palette. For example, with **Contiguous** deselected, if the foreground color is red and you click a yellow pixel, all yellow pixels in the entire image will change to red, regardless of whether they adjoin or not.

How to Fill with Patterns

Filling an area with a pattern is a two-step process: First, you define the pattern to use, and then you specify its use as a fill. The pattern is tiled across the image to complete the effect. Patterned fills are useful for decorative effects, as well as for testing how a seamless tile will work in a preliminary Web page design.

Begin

1 Select the Pattern Area

With the image file you want to modify open onscreen, select the **Marquee** tool in the toolbox. Drag a square or rectangular marquee in the image to define the pattern area.

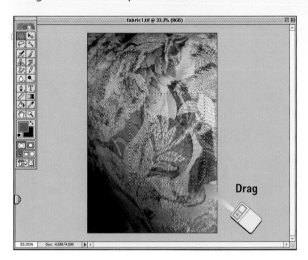

Drag

2 Define the Pattern

Choose **Edit, Define Pattern** to save the selected area as a pattern. (Actually, the selected area is placed on the Clipboard for your use later in this task.) Now press ⌘+D (**Ctrl+D** in Windows) to deselect the area.

Click

3 Select the Paint Bucket Tool

Double-click the **Paint Bucket** tool in the toolbox to select the tool and open the **Paint Bucket Options** palette.

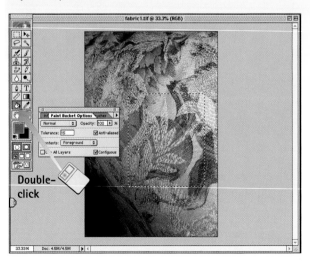

Double-click

4 Set the Options Palette

In the **Paint Bucket Options** palette, select **Pattern** from the **Contents** drop-down list. Set the **Opacity**, **Tolerance**, and other settings as desired. The effect shown in the next step uses an **Opacity** setting of **100** and a **Tolerance** setting of **15**. Refer to Task 7, "How to Fill with the Paint Bucket," for details on setting tolerances and opacity.

5 Apply the Effect

Choose **Select, Deselect** to deselect the marquee selection created in Step 1. Click once in the image area to fill the entire image with the repeating pattern. In this case, the **Tolerance** setting of **15** was adequate for filling the entire screen.

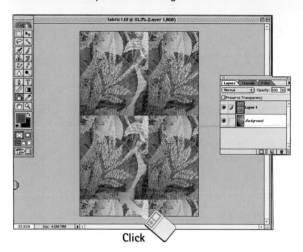

Click

End

How-To Hints

Use the Fill Command

You also can apply a pattern to an image by choosing **Edit, Fill**. In the **Fill** dialog box that opens, select **Pattern** from the **Use** drop-down list and set the **Opacity** and **Mode** options as desired.

How to Apply Gradients

A *gradient* is a fill that gradually blends two or more colors together. These color blends can be applied in circular-shaped, diamond-shaped, and cone-shaped gradients, as well as standard linear and bar shapes. When you apply a gradient, it expands to fill the entire selected area. Gradients are useful as background fills behind an object, as well as in layer masks to fade out an image (see Part 11, Task 6 for details on layer masks).

Begin

1 Select the Fill Area

Open the image file you want to work with. If necessary, select the area to be filled with the gradient. If no area is selected, Photoshop fills the entire image with the gradient effect. In this example, the background behind the moth has been selected.

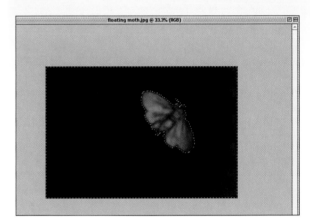

2 Select Gradient Type

Click and hold the **Gradient** tool in the toolbox and select the **Linear, Radial, Angle, Reflected,** or **Diamond Gradient** tool. After you select a tool, double-click the tool to open the **Options** palette for that particular tool.

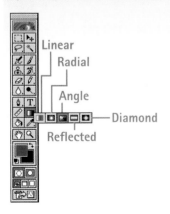

3 Set Foreground/Background Colors

By default, the **Gradient** tool applies its effect using the current foreground and background colors. In the toolbox, click either the **Foreground** or **Background** color swatch and select the desired gradient colors using the **Color Picker** dialog box that appears.

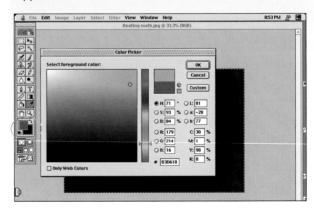

4 Set the Options Settings

The **Options** palette shows a thumbnail example of the gradient effect to be applied. Set the **Opacity** as desired, choosing a setting of less than 100 to create a transparent gradient. Make sure that the **Gradient** option is set to **Foreground to Background**. Leave the **Transparency** check box de-selected and check the **Dither** check box if you want to reduce banding in the gradient. Finally, select the **Reverse** check box to switch the colors in the gradient. Click **OK**.

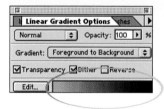

5 Apply the Effect

Position the cursor in the image where you want the gradient to start. Click and drag, releasing the mouse to apply the effect. Remember that the gradient will cover the entire image; the point at which you release the mouse determines the end of the gradient transition. Choose **Select, Deselect** to complete the effect.

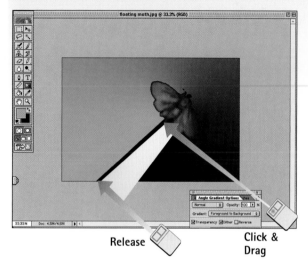

Release   Click & Drag

End

How-To Hints

Dither for Smoother Gradients
Enable the **Dither** check box in the **Options** palette to smooth the gradient effect.

Tweak a Gradient
If you are not satisfied with the angle or tone break, drag again to reapply the gradient, overwriting the previous attempt. This works only if the **Mode** in the **Options** palette is set to **Normal** *and* **Opacity** is set to **100**.

How to Create Custom Gradients

Building a custom gradient in Photoshop involves defining the number of colors in the gradient, as well as how they fade and transition between each other. It also is possible to build transparency into the gradient, which allows the layers below the current layer to show through the gradient. Gradients are similar to custom brushes in that you customize them for each image. Photoshop lets you create and save custom gradients and add them to the preset list for easy access. After you create a gradient, you can use it with any of the gradient shapes selected from the toolbox.

Begin

1 Open the Gradient Editor

Double-click any of the gradient tools to launch the **Gradient Options** palette. Click the **Edit** button to open the **Gradient Editor** dialog box.

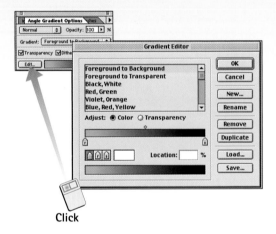

Click

2 Select a Preset

From the list at the top of the dialog box, select one of the existing gradient presets if you want to use it as a starting point. If not, click the **New** button on the right and provide a name for the gradient you will create in the dialog box that appears.

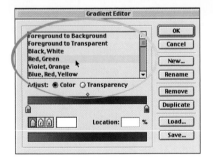

3 Select the Starting Color

Double-click the left color stop in the gradient bar in the **Gradient Editor** to open the **Color Picker**. Select a color and click **OK** to close the **Color Picker**. The new color appears on the left end of the gradient bar, and the gradient is updated.

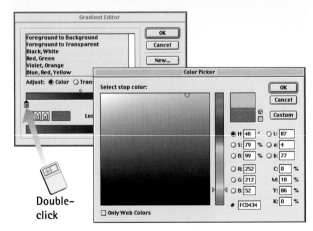

Double-click

4 Select the Ending Color

Double-click the right color stop in the gradient bar in the **Gradient Editor** to open the **Color Picker**. Select a color and click **OK** to close the **Color Picker**. The new color appears at the right end of the gradient bar, and the gradient is updated.

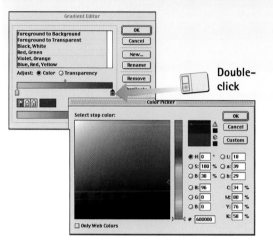

Double-click

5 Set the Break

The *break* in a gradient determines where a 50 percent mix of the two colors occurs. By default, the break is in the middle of the gradient, but you can adjust the placement by dragging the diamond above the gradient bar. By adjusting the break point, you can designate a dominant color for the gradient.

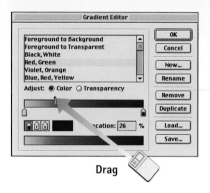

Drag

6 Add Additional Colors

Double-click in the color stop section below the gradient bar to add a third color stop. This action opens the **Color Picker**. Select the third color you want to add to the gradient; click **OK** to close the **Color Picker** and add the color to the gradient. Drag the new color stop as necessary to control the color placement in the gradient. Notice that a new diamond is placed between each color to control the breaks between colors.

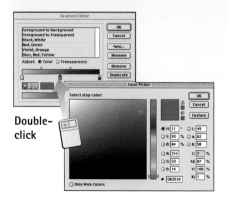

Double-click

7 Save the Gradient

Click **OK** to save the gradient and close the **Gradient Editor**. If you want, you can click the **Save** button to save the gradient as a separate file to be loaded later. When you do this, a **Save As** dialog box opens for you to name the gradient file and specify where it goes.

End

How-To Hints

Using Transparency

You can build transparency areas into the custom gradient to allow the lower layers to show through. Select the **Transparency** radio button in the **Gradient Editor**, select a color stop, and type a value in the **Opacity** field. The results appear in the gradient bar at the bottom of the dialog box.

Task

9

PART

Using Type

*T*here was a time when using text in Photoshop was a pretty bad idea. In the pre-version 2.5 days, there were no layers, History brushes, or multiple undos, so when you placed text on an image, it was there permanently. Kerning or leading was out of the question—and heaven forbid if you had a typo! Unless you were very brave or very stupid, text was the domain of illustration and layout programs.

This began to change when Adobe added layers with version 3.0. Then an enhanced text tool, vertical type, and kerning controls hit the scene. One of the biggest enhancements has been Photoshop's capability to keep text as an editable item at all times. When text was placed as a bitmap, if you misspelled the word, you were out of luck. With editable text, however, you just reopen the dialog box and make the correction.

The tasks in this part profile the primary features for working with type in Photoshop. As a general rule, you still will not want to set large amounts of type in Photoshop (the bitmap nature of the program will hurt readability when compared with vector-based or text-based applications). Keep your use of text to headlines and a few paragraphs, and you'll find that Photoshop's text capabilities are a full-featured option that was well worth the wait. ●

How to Add Type to an Image

When you add text to an image in Photoshop, it is placed on a separate layer. It remains editable at all times—unless you intentionally convert the image to pixels for further editing (as you must if you want to apply filters that work only on raster layers) or integration. When text is added, a new layer is created. The text is the only element in the layer; all other areas are transparent. Photoshop can access all fonts in your system and makes them available through the **Type Tool** dialog box.

Begin

1 Select the Type Tool

With the image open, click the **Type** tool from the Photoshop toolbox. It resides in a pop-out menu with the **Type Mask** tool, the **Vertical Type** tool, and the **Vertical Type Mask** tool. If any of these other tools are active, click and hold the active tool in the toolbox to activate the pop-out menu, and then select the **Type** tool.

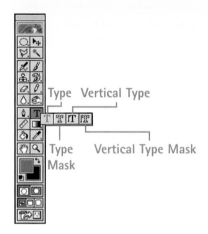

2 Place the Text Starting Point

Move the mouse pointer into the image area and click to set the text entry point. This action opens the **Type Tool** dialog box.

Click

3 Select the Font

Choose a typeface from the **Font** pop-up menu and a typestyle (bold, oblique/italic, and so on) from the submenu. You also can apply an artificial bold and italic effect in this area. The "artificial," or "faux," italic and bold settings exist because the new type engine (in Photoshop version 5 and later) doesn't display bold and italic versions of fonts that do not have these characteristics built in.

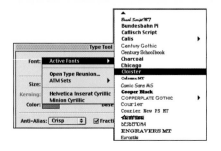

4 Set Parameters

Set the font size, *kerning* (spacing between individual pairs of letters), *tracking* (spacing between entire lines of letters), *baseline shift* (whether the letters sit on an invisible baseline or "float" above or below it), and type color in the next section. You can align the text to the left, center, or right (in relation to the entry point) by clicking one of the three icons at the far right of the dialog box.

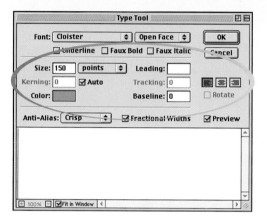

5 Type Text

Click in the text entry area of the dialog box and type the text you want to add to the image. Notice that the text you type appears in the main image window as well, reflecting all the type parameters you've selected. You can reposition the text on the image by clicking and dragging it at any time, even with the **Type Tool** dialog box still open.

6 Set Anti-Alias

Click the **Anti-Alias** pop-up menu and select the sharpness of the type. The sharpness of the image, the kind of background the text sits on, and your overall intentions will determine this setting. Use your eye to judge type for the Web. For print, try to stay with the **Strong** or **Crisp** option, unless you want a softer effect. Click **OK** to create the type layer on the image.

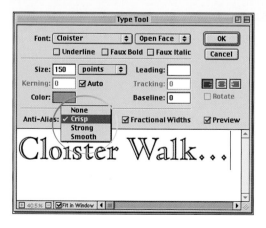

7 Edit the Type

The type is represented as a separate layer on the image, denoted as a type layer by the T icon in the **Layers** palette. Double-click the layer tile at any time to reopen the **Type Tool** dialog box and modify the text.

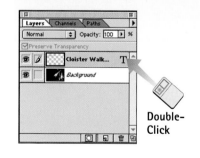

Double-Click

End

How to Place Vertical Type

Vertical type is text that is arranged in a descending vertical column down the image. This task explains how to create a type layer that features this effect, outlining the various alignment options and text controls available to you.

Begin

1 Select the Vertical Type Tool

With the image open, select the **Vertical Type** tool from the Photoshop toolbox. It resides in a pop-out menu with the **Type** tool, the **Type Mask** tool, and the **Vertical Type Mask** tool. If any of these other tools are active, click and hold the active tool to activate the pop-out menu and then select the **Vertical Type** tool.

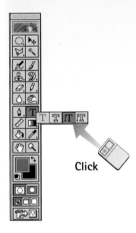

Click

2 Place the Text Starting Point

Move the cursor into the image area and click to set the text entry point. This action opens the **Type Tool** dialog box.

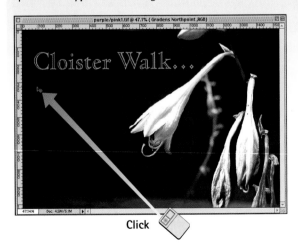

Click

3 Set Parameters

Select the font and font attributes for the text. Refer to Task 1 for details about the **Font** area of the **Type Tool** dialog box.

4 Define Type Orientation

The text can extend down, up, or centered on the text entry point. Click the button that represents the orientation you want. Depending on the button you click, the text will flow up, down, or be centered from where you clicked the text tool in the image in Step 2.

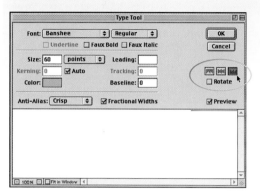

5 Enter Text

Click in the text entry area of the dialog box and type the text you want to add to the image. As you type, notice that the text appears in the image area also. You can reposition the text on the image by dragging it at any time, even with the **Type Tool** dialog box still open. Click **OK** to place the text and create the text layer.

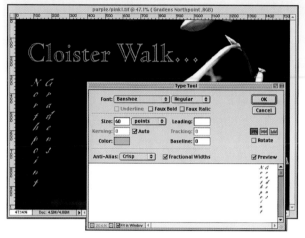

End

How-To Hints

Use the Rotate Check Box

Vertical text can be oriented with the character baseline running horizontally or vertically. The baseline is horizontal by default, but you can set it to vertical by enabling the **Rotate** check box. Be careful with a vertical baseline; it can make text harder to read.

Rendering Text

To change a type layer to pixels, choose **Layer, Type, Render Layer**. Note that you cannot edit text as text after you render the layer as pixels.

No Multiple Colors

About the only thing the Photoshop **Type** tool does not let you do is specify multiple colors. Changing the color spec changes the color of *all* the text in the **Type Tool** dialog box. You must either create separate text layers for multiple colors, or render the layer and color the pixels. If you render the layer, be sure to enable the **Preserve Transparency** check box, which enables you to paint the text shapes with a standard brush without distorting the outlines.

How to Create 3D Text

3D text refers to type that includes shading or modeling to create a three-dimensional effect on the page or image. These effects can include drop shadows, embossing, and other impressive options. This current task is specific to creating great-looking type.

1 Create the Text

Follow the instructions in Task 1 or 2 to create a text layer. When you have created the text layer, verify its existence by checking the **Layers** palette.

2 Select Bevel and Emboss Effects

Choose **Layer, Effects, Bevel and Emboss** to launch the **Effects** dialog box. Make sure that the **Preview** and **Apply** check boxes are enabled.

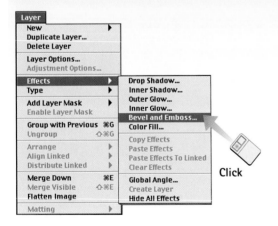

Click

3 Select the Bevel Style

From the **Style** pop-up menu, select the desired bevel style. Options are **Outer Bevel, Inner Bevel, Emboss,** and **Pillow Emboss.** Because the **Preview** check box is enabled, you can select each option and see the results in the main image window.

4 Set the Angle

The **Angle** option determines the angle at which the "light" falls on the text. The angle setting determines the shadows and highlights on the text. Click the arrow to the right of the **Angle** box. In the compass box that pops up, drag the angle line to rotate to the desired angle.

5 Set the Depth

The **Depth** option determines the thickness of the bevel. The "proper" thickness depends on the font size selected and the overall resolution of the image. Click the arrow to the right of the **Depth** box; drag the resulting slider to set the proper depth. Then experiment with the **Up** and **Down** radio buttons to reverse the apparent light angle.

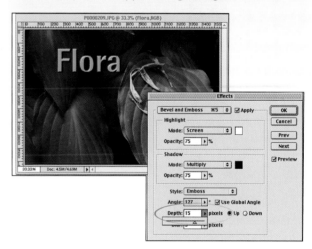

6 Set the Blur

Blur is different from depth in that blur determines the softness of the effect rather than the size. Click the arrow to the right of the **Blur** box; drag the resulting slider to set the appropriate amount of blur for your text.

7 Tweak the Highlights and Shadows

If necessary, you can change the color for the highlight and shadow; you also can set the opacity and mode. Click the color swatches in the **Effects** dialog box to open the **Color Picker**, from which you can select a new color. Select the mode and opacity from the **Mode** and **Opacity** list boxes.

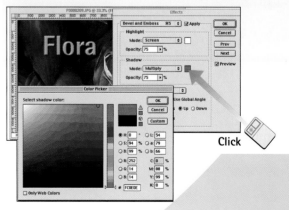

Click

End

How to Build Filtered Text Effects

Instead of placing text as straightforward characters, you may want the text to appear as lightened or darkened areas of the image itself. You also can apply a textured effect to delineate the text characters. This task uses Photoshop filters to modify a text selection mask, creating an effect that integrates the text with the background image. In addition to filters, you can use color shifts, contrast changes, and texture effects when applying the filtering technique. Part 13, "Special Effects," introduces some of the techniques available.

Begin

1 Duplicate the Target Layer

Open the image file and determine the layer that will serve as the background for the effect. Select that layer in the **Layers** palette and choose **Duplicate Layer** from the palette menu. After the **Duplicate Layer** dialog box opens, provide a name for the layer you are creating and click **OK**.

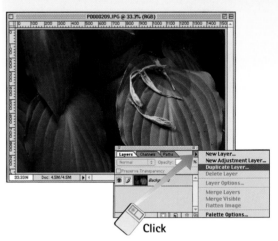

Click

2 Select the Type Mask Tool

Select the **Type Mask** tool from the Photoshop toolbox. It resides in a pop-out menu with the **Type** tool, the **Vertical Type** tool, and the **Vertical Type Mask** tool. If any of these other tools are active, click the active tool to activate the pop-out menu and then select the **Type Mask** tool.

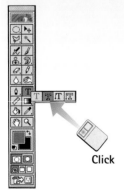

Click

3 Place the Text Starting Point

Move the cursor into the image area and click to set the text entry point. This action opens the **Type Tool** dialog box.

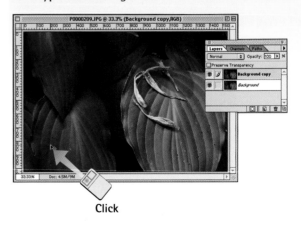

Click

4 Set Parameters

Set the font and font attributes for the text you want to add to the image. For filtered text effects, "fat" typefaces in fairly large point sizes (20 points or larger) work best. Refer to Task 1 or 2 for details about setting these options in the **Type Tool** dialog box.

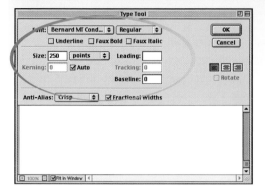

5 Enter Text

Type the text in the bottom pane of the dialog box. Because the **Type Mask** tool creates a *text selection* rather than a *text layer,* you do not see a preview of what you are building. Click the **OK** button to create the selection (the "text" appears in the image in a kind of running-lights, marquee fashion). If the size of the text is wrong, click the **Type Mask** tool anywhere in the image to deselect the text selection and reopen the **Type Tool** dialog box.

6 Invert the Selection

Choose **Select, Inverse** to select the background around the text selection. Press **Delete** to delete the selection (that is, to delete all the background *except* the text). At this point, the text portion of the background is the only part of the image that remains visible as it sits over the transparent image layer.

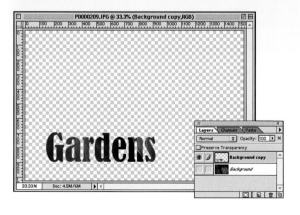

7 Apply a Filter

Open the **Layers** palette. Make sure that the text layer is selected and that the **Preserve Transparency** check box is enabled. From the **Filters** menu, select any of Photoshop's filters. This example uses the Bas Relief filter (**Filter, Sketch, Bas Relief**) set at **Detail = 8** and **Smoothness = 2**. Click **OK** to apply the effect.

End

How to Build a Text Character Brush

You can use any graphic or portion of an image as a custom brush. Photoshop looks at a brush shape as black or grayscale; the shades of gray indicate various levels of transparency. Any colors in the brush shape are read as grayscale. This task looks at creating a brush with text characters that you can apply with a click, like a rubber stamp. You also can apply the effect repeatedly to create a pattern.

Begin

1 Create a New File

Choose **File, New** to create a new file. In the **New** dialog box that appears, set the dimensions of the canvas large enough to accommodate the brush size you want to create.

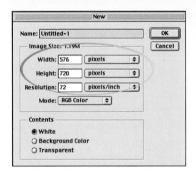

2 Create Text

Select the **Type** tool from the toolbox and use the **Type Tool** dialog box to create the desired text. Use black as the text color. Refer to Task 1 or 2, earlier in this part, for help.

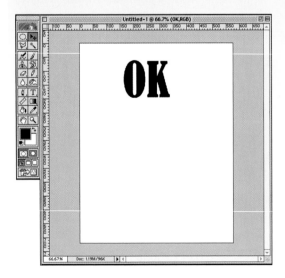

3 Select the Text

Click the **Marquee** tool in the toolbox (select the **Rectangular Marquee** tool from the pop-out list if it is not already selected) and drag a rectangle around the text to select it.

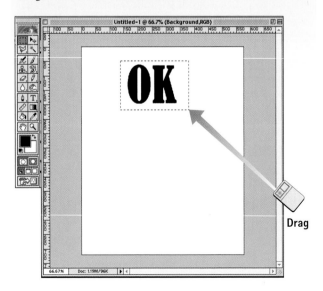

Drag

4 Define the Brush

Open the **Brushes** palette by choosing **Window, Show Brushes**. Select the text and choose **Define Brush** from the Brushes palette menu. The new **OK** brush is added to the bottom of the **Brushes** palette.

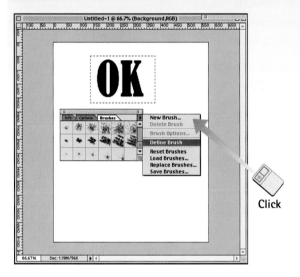

Click

5 Set the Spacing

Double-click the new brush in the **Brushes** palette to launch the **Brush Options** dialog box. The **Spacing** option determines whether the brush paints in a smooth line or in broken strokes. Increase this percentage to increase the readability of the individual brushstrokes.

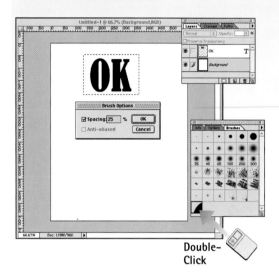

Double-Click

6 Select and Use the Brush

In the **Layers** palette, click the **Background** layer tile to make that the active layer. Click the **Paintbrush** tool in the toolbox and select the brush you just created from the **Brushes** palette. Click once to apply a clean outline of the text; drag to layer the effect.

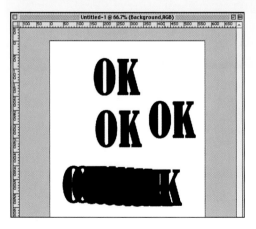

How-To Hints

Limited AntiAlias

Because of memory restrictions, the **Anti-aliased** option is not available for larger images.

Brush Sizes

You can create brushes of up to 1,000 pixels in height and width. Use shades of gray to build in custom transparency to the brush shape. Note that large custom brushes are cropped in the **Brushes** palette, so that only a portion of the design is visible. In the example in Step 5, the brush shape shown in the seventh row is actually the top-left corner of the **OK** brush you created.

End

How to Position Text on a Curve

To be honest, Illustrator and FreeHand can position text on a curved baseline so much better than Photoshop that I hesitate to include this task. But people are always looking for a way to do everything in Photoshop, so if you don't have Illustrator at your disposal, the technique in this task will work in a pinch. This approach involves placing each character by hand; it works very well for a few words or perhaps a sentence. It can get tedious very fast if you work with large blocks of text and is not recommended for such purposes.

Begin

1 Create the Text

Create the text you want to use. Refer to Task 1 or 2, earlier in this part, for help. Keep the text to a single line; if you must use multiple lines, double the leading to allow for adequate line spacing. In addition, increase the space between letters to simplify the selection of the characters later. To increase spacing, highlight the text in the text entry field of the **Type Tool** dialog box and increase the value in the **Tracking** field.

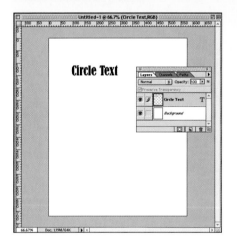

2 Render the Text

Choose **Layer, Text, Render Layer** to convert the text from characters to pixels.

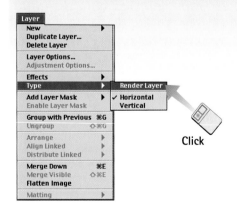

Click

3 Create a New Guide Layer

Open the **Layers** palette by choosing **Window, Show Layers**. From the **Layers** palette menu, choose **New Layer**. In the dialog box that appears, click **OK** to create a new layer on which you will create the circular path guide.

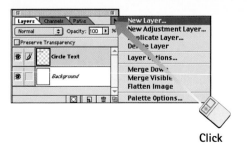

Click

4 Create a Circular Selection

Click and hold the **Marquee** tool in the toolbox. From the pop-out menu, select the **Elliptical Marquee** tool. Drag out a circle or oval that will serve as the path guide along which you will place your text. (**Hint:** If you want a custom-shaped path guide, use the **Pen** tool and the **Paths** palette to draw the more complex shape.)

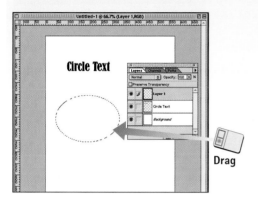

Drag

5 Stroke the Selection

With the new layer active, choose **Edit, Stroke** to open the **Stroke** dialog box. Specify a stroke width and color so that you can see the stroke clearly against your image. Note that the term *stroke* refers to drawing an outline around the object.

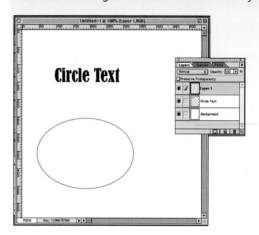

6 Position the Letters

In the **Layers** palette, switch to the text layer (the layer that contains the rendered text). Choose the **Rectangular Marquee** tool from the toolbox and drag a selection around the first letter in the text. Choose **Edit, Transform, Rotate**, place the mouse pointer inside the transform cage, and drag the character into position against the elliptical guide. Click and drag a corner handle to rotate the shape into position. When the character is in position, press **Enter/Return** to apply the effect. Repeat this step for all the characters.

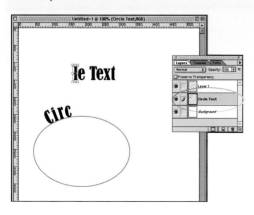

7 Remove the Guide Layer

In the **Layers** palette, select the guide layer tile. From the palette menu, select **Delete Layer** to delete the guide layer and complete the effect.

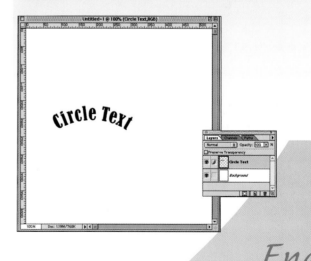

End

Task

PART 10

Using Paths

*P*aths offer the capability to outline shapes or areas within Photoshop files. You then can convert the paths into selections, fill the paths with color, or outline the paths as borders.

Paths offer many advantages. They add very little to the overall file size, and they use standard vector controls such as Bezier curves, points, and direction handles. If you know how to create curved segments in Adobe Illustrator or Macromedia FreeHand, you will catch on to the Photoshop path controls very quickly.

Other advantages to paths include the flexibility of being able to export them to other files and programs. If you use the **Paths** palette, you can drag paths from the palette for one image window into another open window (an easy way to move paths between Photoshop files). In addition, you can export individual paths as `.ai` files, which you can open in Illustrator, FreeHand, and many other programs that support vector graphics. Doing so gives you more flexibility in illustration and layout programs when mixing vector graphics with the bitmapped images created or modified in Photoshop. ●

How to Create a Straight-Edge Path

You can use paths to define an image area, which you then can select, fill, or outline. Paths are especially valuable for graphic shapes you may want to select repeatedly. You create a path using the **Pen** tool: You click points that are connected automatically with line segments. This task begins by creating a simple path with straight-line segments; later tasks show you how to create more complex path shapes.

Begin

1 Open the File

Choose **File**, **Open** to launch the desired file.

2 Select the Pen Tool

Select the **Pen** tool from the toolbox (you may have to select it from the pop-out menu of tools that appears after you click this button in the toolbox).

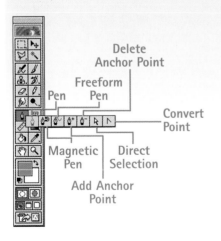

Delete Anchor Point

Freeform Pen

Pen

Convert Point

Magnetic Pen

Direct Selection

Add Anchor Point

3 Place the First Point

Position the pen over the image area at the spot where you want to start the path. Click once to place an anchor point.

Click

4 Place Additional Points

Click additional points as needed to complete the path. Notice that a straight line is drawn between the points you click with the **Pen** tool.

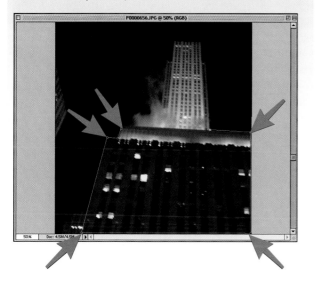

5 Close the Path

Place the last point over the starting point to close the path. A circle appears next to the Pen tool when the tool is positioned properly.

6 Open the Paths Palette

Choose **Window, Show Paths** to launch the **Paths** palette. Double-click the tile for the path you just created (the tile has the title **Work Path**). The **Save Path** dialog box opens. Type a name for the path and click **OK** to save the path.

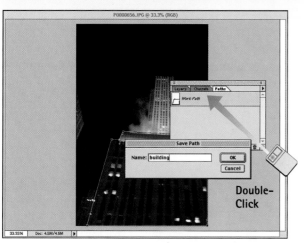

Double-Click

How-To Hints

Deleting Paths

Press the **Delete** key twice to delete the path you are currently drawing. Alternatively, select **Delete Path** from the **Paths** palette menu to delete a selected path or segment.

Duplicating Paths

Select **Duplicate Paths** from the **Paths** palette menu to copy a selected path.

End

How to Create a Curved Path

Although the straight-line paths created in Task 1 are good for basic shapes, you will no doubt want to create paths with curved lines as well. This task shows how to draw paths with curved segments, enabling you to create more complex and detailed paths.

Begin

1 Open the File

Choose **File, Open** to launch the desired file. Select the **Pen** tool from the toolbox (you may have to select it from the pop-out menu that appears after you click the tool in the toolbox).

Click

2 Place the First Point

Position the pen over the image area at the spot where you want to start the path. Click once to place an anchor point.

Click

3 Create the First Curved Segment

Click and drag while placing the second point to create a curved path segment. Two handles appear out of the second point as you drag, showing the direction of the curve.

Click & Drag

4 Modify the Curve

Press and hold the ⌘ key (Mac users) or Ctrl key (Windows users) to change the Pen cursor into the **Direct Selection** tool. Click and drag either of the handles to change the shape of the curve.

Click & Drag

5 Complete the Path

Continue adding points to create additional straight or curved segments as necessary. Click the first point again to close the path, if desired.

6 Save and Name the Path

Open the **Paths** palette by choosing **Window, Show Paths**. In the palette, double-click the tile for the path you just created (the tile has the name **Work Path**). In the **Save Path** dialog box that appears, type a name for the path and click **OK** to save the path.

Double-Click

How-To Hints

Editing Curved Segments

Instead of editing each curved segment as you make it, you may find it easier to approximate all the curve points and fine-tune the segments all at once. When you work this way, you can select the **Direct Selection** tool directly from the toolbox instead of pressing the ⌘/**Ctrl** key as you did in Step 4.

End

TASK *3*

How to Edit a Path

Photoshop offers a number of ways to edit a path; you can add, subtract, or move points with ease. You can edit a path at any time—as you're making it or later in the process. This task shows all the ways to edit a path, enabling you to pick and choose the options applicable to your project.

Begin

1 Open the File with the Path

Choose **File, Open** to launch the file containing the path you want to edit.

2 Select the Path

Choose **Window, Show Paths** to launch the **Paths** palette. Click the title of the desired path to select it. The path becomes visible in the image window as you highlight it.

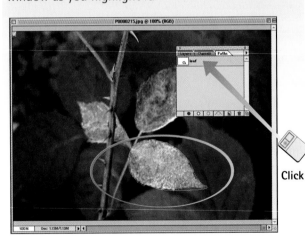

Click

3 Move a Point

Click the **Direct Selection** tool in the toolbox. Click in the middle of a line segment to show the points on the path. Click and drag a point to move it. If the point is related to a curved segment, handles appear when you select the point, enabling you to modify the curve.

Drag

4 Move Multiple Points

To move multiple points as a group, select the **Direct Selection** tool and show the points in the path, as described in Step 3. After clicking the first point, press and hold the **Shift** key and click additional points (the points darken to show that they are selected). When multiple points are selected, click and drag to move them as a group.

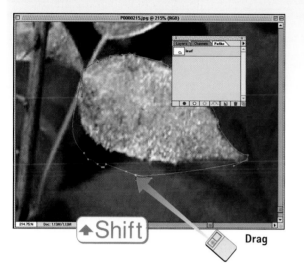

↑Shift
Drag

5 Add a Point

To add a point to a path, begin by selecting the **Add Anchor Point** tool from the **Pen** tool pop-out menu in the toolbox. Select the path you want to edit from the **Paths** palette, position the cursor over the path segment, and click to add a new point. Click and drag to create a point with a curved path segment.

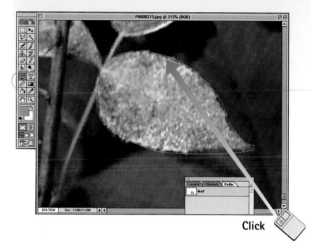

Click

6 Delete a Point

To delete a point from a path, begin by selecting the **Delete Anchor Point** tool from the **Pen** tool pop-out menu in the toolbox. Select the path you want to edit from the **Paths** palette, position the cursor over the point to be removed, and click to delete.

Click

7 Convert an Anchor Point

A complex path consists of both curved and straight-line segments, which are determined by smooth and corner anchor points, respectively. To convert between smooth and corner points, select the **Convert Anchor Point** tool and position it over the point to be converted. Click to convert a smooth point to a corner point; click and drag to convert a corner point to a smooth point.

How to Convert a Path to a Selection

One of the primary reasons for creating a path is to convert it to a selection. You can convert a path to a selection as long as the path is available. Because paths take less disk space to save than do selections, you probably shouldn't save a selection when you can save the path.

Begin

1 Open the File

Choose **File, Open** to launch the desired file.

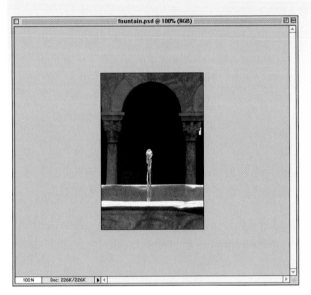

2 Create the Path

Use any of the methods described so far to create a path.

3 Choose Make Selection

Choose **Window, Show Paths** to launch the **Paths** palette. With the path selected, choose **Make Selection** from the palette menu. The **Make Selection** dialog box opens.

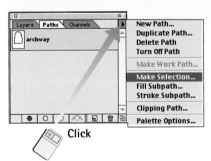

4 Enter the Feather Radius

Enable the **Anti-aliased** check box and enter a feather amount if you want a selection with soft edges (or of you are making a selection around fine details such as hair). Click **OK** to make the selection.

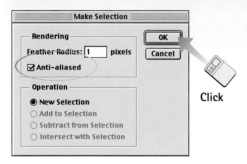

Click

5 Deselect the Path

From the **Paths** palette menu, choose **Turn Off Path** to hide the displayed path and show only the selection.

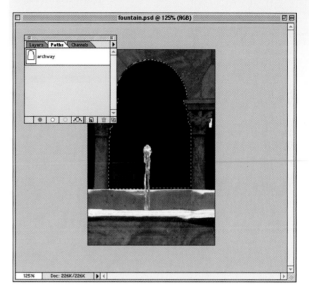

End

How-To Hints

Combining Selections

You can use paths to create selections that interact with existing selections, as determined by the **Operation** section of the **Make Selection** dialog box. If no selection is active in the image area when you choose **Make Selection,** only the **New Selection** radio button is available. If another selection is active when you open this dialog box, you can choose to add to, subtract from, or intersect the path selection with the current one.

Convert a Selection to a Path

If an area already is selected, you easily can convert the selection line to a path. With a selection active, select **Make Work Path** from the **Paths** palette menu, select a tolerance level, and click **OK**. If the result is a path with too many points, undo the conversion and set a higher tolerance level. The result is a work path you can save and name as you want.

How to Stroke Paths

Stroking a path draws an outline around a selected path. This capability is useful for outlining a rectangle for a text box, building buttons for the Web, or outlining letter forms you have saved as paths. You can create the outline by using any of Photoshop's painting or drawing tools for a wide range of effects. You can even specify the brush size, opacity, and blending mode for full control over the final result.

Begin

1 Open the File

Choose **File, Open** to launch the desired file.

2 Create or Select a Path

Use any of the methods described so far to create a path. In this example, I used the **Polygonal Lasso** tool to create a path around the figure in the image area.

3 Configure the Stroke Tool

Double-click the tool you want to use to stroke the path. In the **Options** palette that appears for that tool, configure the tool as desired. Choose **Window, Show Brushes** to open the **Brushes** palette. Then select a brush size for the tool you're using.

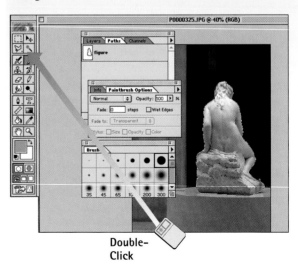

Double-Click

4 Select the Stroke Path

If it's not already open, choose **Window, Show Paths** to launch the **Paths** palette. With the desired path active, select **Stroke Path** from the palette menu. (If the path is not named, the menu option reads **Stroke Subpath**.) The **Stroke Path** dialog box opens.

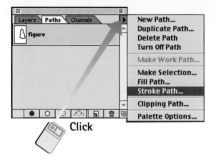

Click

5 Stroke the Path

The tool you configured in Step 3 should be selected in the **Stroke Path** dialog box when it opens. If you want to use a different tool, select it from the **Tool** drop-down list and click **OK**. A line will be drawn, in the current foreground color, along the path, using the tool you selected, and applying the current settings for that particular tool.

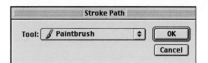

6 Deselect the Path

From the **Paths** palette menu, choose **Turn Off Path** to deselect the path and show the final result.

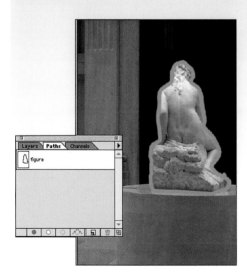

How-To Hints

Make an Object Glow

To create an easy glow effect using the stroking method, select the **Airbrush** tool as the stroke tool and stroke the path with a large brush at a low opacity setting. Stroke the path several more times, reducing the brush size and increasing the opacity to build up a glowing effect.

End

How to Fill Paths

Another common use of paths is to fill them with a specific color (which you set in the **Foreground** or **Background** swatch in the toolbox). You also can make a selection as described in Part 3, "Selection Techniques," and then fill the selection, but this just eliminates the step of converting the path to a selection. You already know that it is better to save your selections as paths rather than as selections.

Begin

1 Open the File

Choose **File, Open** to launch the desired file.

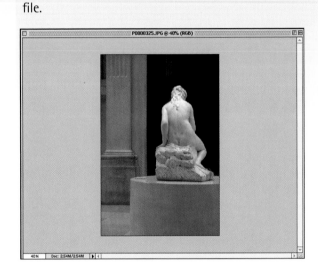

2 Create or Select the Path

Use any of the methods described so far to create a path. In this example, I used the **Magnetic Pen** tool to create a path around the figure in the image area.

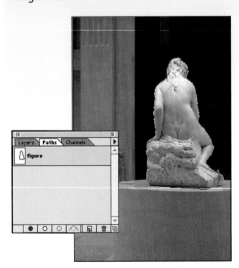

3 Specify the Foreground Color

Click the **Foreground** color swatch in the toolbox to launch the **Color Picker**. Select a color to be used for the fill and click **OK**.

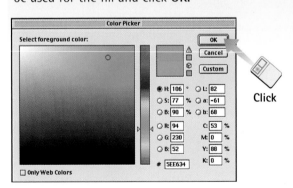

Click

4 Select the Fill Path

If it's not already open, choose **Window, Show Paths** to launch the **Paths** palette. Choose **Fill Path** from the palette menu (the menu option is labeled **Fill Subpath** if the path has not been named). The **Fill Path** dialog box opens.

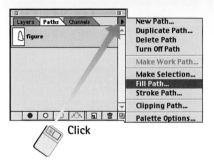

Click

5 Set Fill Contents

From the **Use** drop-down list, select **Foreground Color**. This option specifies the color or pattern you want to use to fill the area in the image that is outlined by the path.

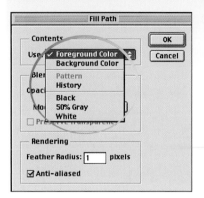

6 Set Blending and Feathering

Modify the **Opacity** and **Feather Radius** values to add transparency or a soft edge to the fill.

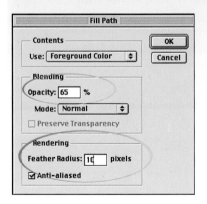

7 Fill the Path

Click **OK** to fill the path. Deselect the path (from the **Paths** palette menu, choose **Turn Off Path**) to view the results clearly.

End

How to Create Clipping Paths

Clipping paths refer to a method of exporting a file for use in a vector or layout application in a format that masks out part of the image. The most common use is to drop out the background in a product shot so that only the product object is visible. Although the file looks normal in Photoshop, when it is placed in the new application, everything not contained in the path is masked out.

Begin

1 Open the File

Choose **File, Open** to launch the desired file.

2 Create and Name the Path

Use any of the methods described so far to create a path. In the **Paths** palette, double-click the **Work Path** file and name the path you just created.

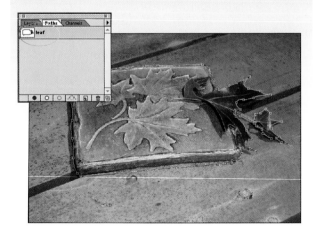

3 Select the Clipping Path

Select **Clipping Path** from the **Paths** palette menu to launch the **Clipping Path** dialog box. From the **Path** drop-down list, choose the path you want to use for the clipping path. In this example, you have only two options: **None** and the path you selected and named in Step 2.

4 Set the Flatness

Set the **Flatness** level to **0.2** and click **OK** to set the clipping path. The **Flatness** setting affects how "smooth" the path will be. The pathname in the **Paths** palette appears in an outlined font to show that a clipping path has been applied using that path.

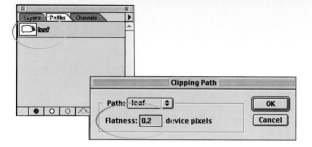

5 Save the File as EPS

To preserve the clipping path along with the file so that it can be imported into a layout or illustration program, you must save the file in either the **.TIFF** or **.EPS** format. To save it as an EPS file, choose **File, Save As** to save a copy of the file. From the **Format** drop-down list in the **Save As** dialog box, select **Photoshop EPS** or **Photoshop DCS**, type a new name for the file, and click **Save**. (Note that you can save a file in DCS format only if the color mode for the file is CMYK.)

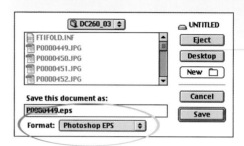

6 Set Preview Options

Set DCS or EPS preview options in the **EPS Options** dialog box that appears and click **OK** to save the file.

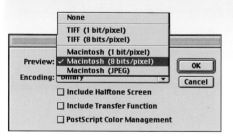

End

How-To Hints

Watch the Flatness

If the resulting path creates printing or PostScript errors, reset the clipping path using a higher **Flatness** setting (as described in Step 4). A higher **Flatness** setting creates fewer points when the path is interpreted by the printer, which eliminates most printing errors.

How to Export Paths to Illustrator

Because paths are PostScript outlines, they work very well in Adobe Illustrator. A common practice is to open an image in Photoshop, define a path, and then export that path to Illustrator to add various graphic effects. You then can rasterize the graphics back into Photoshop and integrate them into the original image design.

Begin

1 Open the File

Choose **File, Open** to launch the desired file.

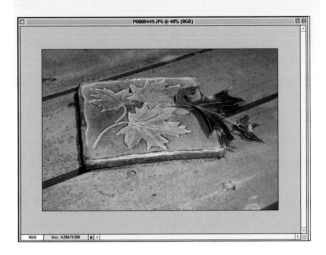

2 Create or Select the Path

Use any of the methods described so far to create a path. In this example, I used the **Pen** tool to create a path around the figure in the image area.

3 Choose the Export Command

Choose **File, Export, Paths to Illustrator**. In the dialog box that appears, select the desired path from the **Write** drop-down list.

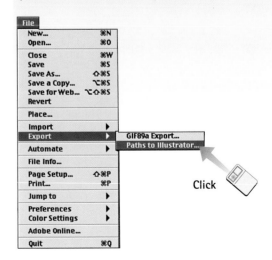

Click

4 Name the New File

Give the file you are creating a name in the **Export Paths to File** box and click **Save** to create a new Illustrator file.

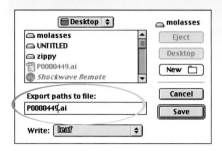

5 Launch Illustrator

Launch Adobe Illustrator. Choose **File, Open** and open the file you created in Step 4. Choose **Edit, Select All** to view the path and its points.

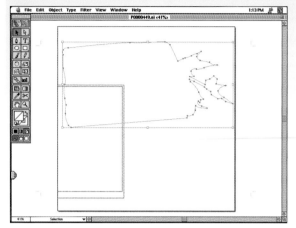

End

How-To Hints

Use Place for a Template

To view the path in Illustrator in relation to the source image, choose **File, Place** in Illustrator and select the source image from the dialog box that appears. This action places the original Photoshop image in Illustrator for your preview and reference purposes.

Task

11

Working with Layers

Layers deliver flexibility, color control, and silhouetting options that factor into most intermediate to advanced image-editing tasks. It's hard to imagine doing any sort of image montage or text integration without taking advantage of layers. In some cases, it's just impossible.

Layers isolate parts of an image in a separate, *um... layer*, which you can edit and modify without altering the other layers around it. Think of layered sheets of acetate stacked on top of each other. Viewed from the top, they flatten out and show an entire scene, yet they keep the elements separate from each other.

You can reposition layers in the stack to control how different components overlap with each other. You also can hide layers from view or display them with varying levels of transparency. The tasks in this part explore the essentials involved in creating and combining layers, building the foundation for professional image compositing. ●

How to Create and Move Layers

You should create a layer any time you want to isolate an element from the rest of the image. The element can be text, a second image, or an area of flat color. You can create a layer by using the **New Layer** command, by pasting an element, or by duplicating an existing layer. After you create the layer, it appears in the **Layers** palette, named in numerical sequence. To rename a layer, double-click the layer's name in the **Layers** palette and rename it in the dialog box that appears.

Begin

1 Open the File

Choose **File, Open** and select the image file you want to modify.

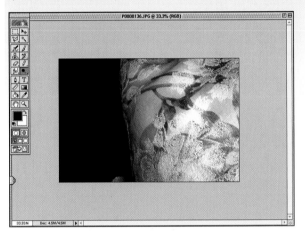

2 Open the Layers Palette

Choose **Window, Show Layers** to open the **Layers** palette.

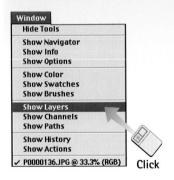

Click

3 Select a New Layer

To create a new layer, choose **Layer, New, Layer.** (Alternatively, select **New Layer** from the **Layers** palette menu.) In the dialog box that appears, name the layer and click **OK.** By default, the layers are given sequential numbers (**Layer 1, Layer 2,** and so on). For this example, create at least two layers. On Layer 2, add some text and format it in a large, bold typeface.

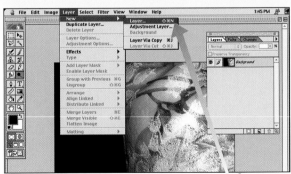

Click

4 Control Layer Visibility

To turn a layer's visibility on and off, look at the **Layers** palette. The far-left column contains boxes with eye icons. Click the box next to the layer you want to control the visibility of to display or hide the eye icon—also called the *visibility icon.*

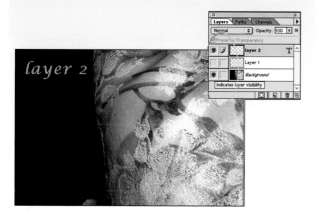

5 Change the Order of the Layers

You can change the order of the layers that form the image. In the **Layers** palette, click the title of the layer you want to move in the stack and drag it to its new position. Moving layers around and changing their order is a very powerful feature. For example, by changing the order of various layers, you can change the apparent order of the objects that reside on these different layers.

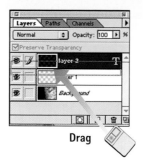

Drag

6 Change Layer Opacity

To make a layer transparent, select the layer in the **Layers** palette to make it the active layer. Adjust the **Opacity** slider at the top of the **Layers** palette until the active layer has the desired degree of opacity. In this example, you can see that the text layer (Layer 2) has been dimmed somewhat using the **Opacity** slider.

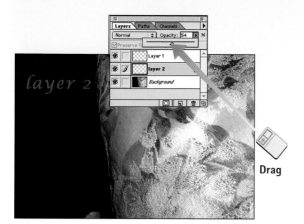

Drag

End

How-To Hints

To Reposition the Background Layer

The **Background** "layer" cannot be repositioned in the layer stack. To move the background, you first must rename it (thus "converting" it from the background/base image to a layer). Double-click the layer's name in the **Layers** palette and enter a new name in the dialog box that appears. (You may want to name it **Layer 0.**) After you rename the ex-background layer, it behaves like any other layer.

Preserving Transparency

You can preserve the transparent areas of a layer by selecting the target layer in the **Layers** palette and placing a check mark in the **Preserve Transparency** check box in the **Layers** palette. This option ensures that you "color within the lines," so to speak, and prevents any painting or editing from registering in the transparent areas.

How to Link Layers

As you accumulate multiple layers in a file, you will want to link certain layers together to preserve alignment or visibility. After you link layers, they all move as a single group as you reposition the multiple layers on the screen—even as they maintain their identities as separate layers. You also can merge linked layers together with a single command, as explained in Task 7 of this part.

Begin

1 Open the File

Choose **File, Open** and select the file you want to edit. This example starts with an image that contains several layers in addition to the basic **Background** "layer." (Note that the **Welcome to Paris** layer contains the text, and the **Taste of Paris copy** layer contains a black shadow of the text.)

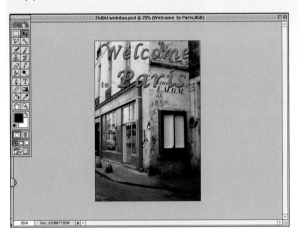

2 Open the Layers Palette

Choose **Window, Show Layers** to open the **Layers** palette.

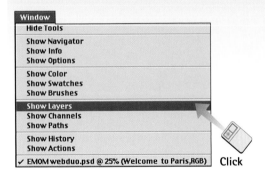

3 Select the Primary Layer

In the **Layers** palette, click the name of the layer to which you want to link other layers. The layer you select here becomes the *primary* layer, or the *active* layer.

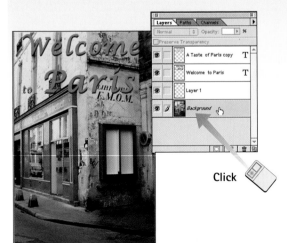

4 Link Secondary Layers

Click in the column to the immediate left of any layers you want to link to the primary layer. A chain icon appears in the column, indicating that the layer is linked to the currently selected layer. In this example, the two text layers are linked to the background; select the **Layer 1** layer and notice that all the chain icons disappear.

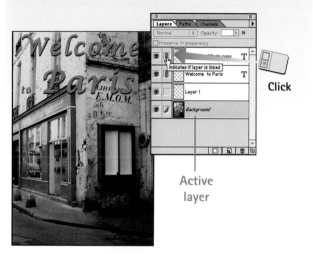

Click

Active layer

5 Unlink Layers

To unlink layers, click the visible chain icons to remove them. When the chain icon is gone, the layer no longer is linked to the currently selected layer.

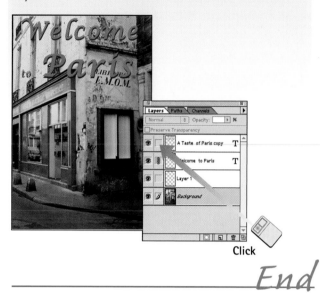

Click

End

How-To Hints

Transforming Linked Layers

Linked layers are treated as a group for more than just movement and alignment. You also can apply the **Transform** command, as outlined in the next task, to modify all the linked layers at once.

How to Transform Layers

When you transform a layer, you modify the position, scale, or proportions of the layer. Transforming a layer is useful for changing the size or placement of a layer, as well as for adding perspective or distortion. You cannot apply the transformation process to the **Background** layer; you must rename that layer before you can transform it. (Double-click the **Background** layer in the **Layers** palette and rename it in the dialog box that appears.) Alternatively, you can duplicate the layer and transform the copy, leaving the original **Background** layer untouched.

1 Open the File

Choose **File, Open** and select the file you want to modify.

2 Open the Layers Palette

Choose **Window, Show Layers** to open the **Layers** palette.

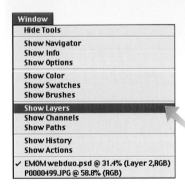

Click

3 Select the Layer to Transform

In the **Layers** palette, click the name of the layer you want to transform. In this example, we select the layer that contains a graphic of a man walking; this man is not part of the original image.

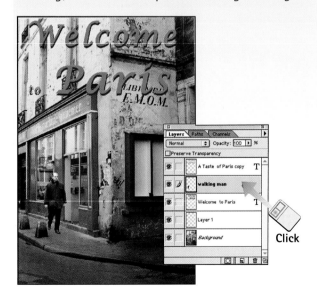

Click

4 Choose Free Transform

Choose **Edit, Free Transform** to begin the transformation process. A bounding box with handles at the sides and the corners surrounds the layer, or the objects on the layer. To transform just a portion of a layer, select the area before choosing **Free Transform** in Step 4. The bounding box covers only the selected area. Background areas left by the transformation will be transparent, allowing lower layers to show through.

Click

5 Modify the Layer

Apply any of the following transformations to the area in the bounding box. **To move:** Place the cursor inside the bounding box and drag. **To scale:** Click and drag a handle (use the **Shift** key to keep the original proportions). **To rotate:** Position the cursor outside the bounding box until it turns into a curved, two-headed arrow and then drag. **To distort freely:** Press and hold ⌘ (Mac users) or **Ctrl** (Windows users) and drag a handle. **To skew:** Press and hold ⌘+**Shift** (Mac users) or **Ctrl+Shift** (Windows users) and drag a side handle. Press **Enter** or **Return** to apply the effect.

End

How-To Hints

Use the Individual Transform Commands

You also can apply individual transform options by choosing **Edit, Transform** and then choosing the transform option from the submenu that appears. This approach constrains the transformation only to the option selected, such as rotating or scaling.

Transform Numerically

You can transform a layer with numeric precision by choosing **Edit, Transform, Numeric**. In the dialog box that appears, adjust the **Position, Scale, Rotation,** and **Skew** options. This approach is especially valuable when you have to repeat the same transformation across multiple unlinked layers.

How to Group Layers

Grouping layers in Photoshop involves linking multiple adjacent layers and using the transparency of the bottom layer of the group as a mask for the other layers. This means that the upper layers are visible only through the "window" created by the transparency of the bottom layer. You also can use a layer mask for the bottom layer in the group instead of actually erasing part of that layer (see Task 6, "How to Add a Layer Mask"). When layers are in a group, the thumbnails in the upper layers in the **Layers** palette are indented, and the line separating the layers is dashed instead of solid.

Begin

1 Open the File

Choose **File, Open** and select the image file you want to modify.

2 Arrange Layers

Choose **Window, Show Layers** to display the **Layers** palette. Arrange all the layers to be grouped so that they are adjacent; make sure that the layer to serve as the mask is positioned at the bottom of the group. In this example, the **Background** layer is at the bottom of the stack, a text layer with the word *foliage* is just above it, a layer with texture is just above that, and the top layer contains the lines drawn with the **Paintbrush** tool.

3 Link Layers

Link the layers of the group together, following the steps in Task 2 of this part. For this example, select the text layer and then click in the column closest to the layer name to make the chain icon appear.

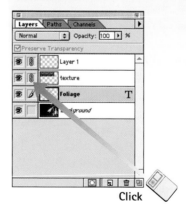

Click

4 Group Layers

Make sure that no layers are linked except for those in the target group. Choose **Layer, Group Linked**. The layers that you linked are now grouped, as you can see by the way the layer names are indented above the bottom, mask layer.

5 Ungroup Layers

If you want to ungroup layers in a group, select the layer to be removed from the group in the **Layers** palette. Choose **Layer, Ungroup**. This action ungroups this layer as well as any grouped layers residing above it.

Click

End

How-To Hints

Setting Opacity and Mode

Set the opacity and mode by highlighting the base layer of the *clipping group* (a group in which the bottom layer acts as a mask for the layers above it) and modifying the **Mode** drop-down list and the **Opacity** slider at the top of the **Layers** palette.

Grouping Shortcuts

You have two methods for adding layers to a group: One is to hold down the **Option** key (Mac users) or **Alt** (Windows users) and position the pointer over the solid line dividing two layers in the **Layers** palette. Click when the pointer changes to two overlapping circles; the two layers are now grouped. The other grouping method is to highlight a layer in the **Layers** palette and choose **Layer, Group with Previous** to group the highlighted layer with the layer before it.

How to Create Adjustment Layers

Adjustment layers are color-correction layers that enable you to adjust the tone or color in an image without altering the content of the layers beneath them. An adjustment layer acts like a filter, altering the appearance of all the layers underneath it— effectively modifying multiple layers at one time. If the result is unsatisfactory, delete or turn off the adjustment layer to return to the previous state. Adjustment layers are like other layers in that you can reposition, hide, or duplicate them in the **Layers** palette.

Begin

1 Open the File

Choose **File, Open** and select the file you want to modify.

2 Open the Layers Palette

Choose **Window, Show Layers** to open the **Layers** palette.

3 Create an Adjustment Layer

Choose **Layer, New, Adjustment Layer** to create a new adjustment layer. The **New Adjustment Layer** dialog box opens.

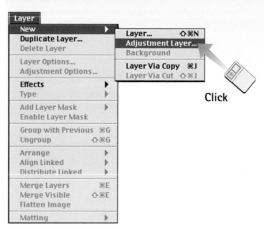

Click

4 Set an Adjustment Type

In the **Name** box, type a name for the layer. From the **Type** drop-down list, select the type of adjustment layer you want to create. This option determines the command used to alter the lower layers. Options are **Levels**, **Curves**, **Brightness/Contrast**, **Color Balance**, **Hue/Saturation**, **Selective Color**, **Channel Mixer**, **Invert**, **Threshold**, and **Posterize**. Click **OK** to create the layer.

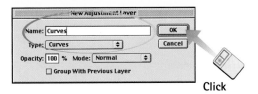

Click

5 Apply the Adjustment

An adjustment dialog box appears based on the **Type** selection you made in Step 4. Adjust the controls to your satisfaction and click **OK** to set the adjustment.

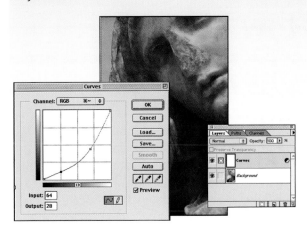

6 Edit the Adjustment

To edit the adjustment settings, double-click the adjustment layer in the **Layers** palette. The adjustment dialog box you saw in Step 5 opens so that you can make further changes.

Double-Click

How-To Hints

Adjustment Layers as Layer Masks

You can paint into an adjustment layer, masking how its effect is applied to the layers underneath. As with other layer masks (described in the following task), painting with black conceals the adjustment effect; painting with white reveals it. With the adjustment layer active in the **Layers** palette, select any paint tool and paint into the image. The color choices convert to grayscale while the adjustment layer is active. The line or area you paint becomes the mask through which the adjustment effect is applied to the remaining layers.

Shortcuts for Adding Adjustment Layers

You also can create an adjustment layer by pressing ⌘ (Mac users) or **Ctrl** (Windows users) as you click the **Create New Layer** button (the one that looks like a dog-eared page) at the bottom of the **Layers** palette.

End

How to Add a Layer Mask

A *layer mask* conceals a portion of a layer without actually deleting it, allowing the lower layers to show through. Erasing the layer mask restores the layer's original appearance so that nothing is lost. The general approach to applying a layer mask is to brush it on using any of the paint tools, controlling the visibility and transparency with grayscale values. As you saw with Quick Mask in Part 3, Task 4, a black value conceals the layer image, white reveals it, and a grayscale value dictates the transparency.

Begin

1 Open the File

Choose **File, Open** and select the image file you want to modify. For this task, I've opened an image with two layers. The lower layer is of an arrangement of foliage and the top layer is of a museum statue. By "painting" in a mask, I'll make it appear as if the statue is surrounded by the foliage and not sitting in the corridor of a museum.

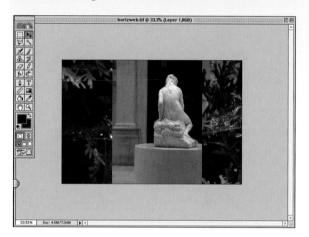

2 Open the Layers Palette

Choose **Window, Show Layers** to open the **Layers** palette.

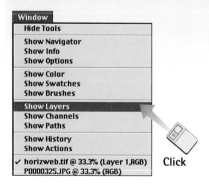

Click

3 Select the Mask Layer

Select the layer to be masked by clicking its name in the **Layers** palette. In this example, we select the layer containing the statue image.

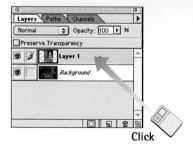

Click

4 Add the Layer Mask

Click the **Add Layer Mask** button at the bottom of the **Layers** palette to add a layer mask to the current layer. The layer mask is indicated in the image tile by a white thumbnail next to the image thumbnail. The border of the new thumbnail is bold, indicating that it is selected.

Add Layer   Add Adjustment
Mask   Layer

5 Paint the Mask

Select the **Paintbrush** tool from the tool-box. Move the cursor into the image area and paint the mask. As you do so, you'll see the current layer disappearing and the lower layer showing through; the thumbnail mask icon is updated to show the current mask. In this example, notice that the museum area behind the statue is being "erased" and the woodsy **Background** layer is showing through.

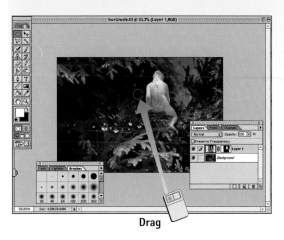

Drag

6 Delete the Mask

To erase or fade part of the mask, change the foreground color to white and repaint the mask. The image layer reappears as you work. To paint in transparency, select a gray foreground color or reduce the **Opacity** setting in the paint tool's **Options** palette. Note that pressing the **X** key enables you to quickly toggle between the foreground and background colors. This is helpful while adjusting the edges of the mask.

Drag

7 Apply the Mask

Because layer masks add significantly to file size, you should consider applying them to the layer when you're confident you will not be making any further changes. To apply the mask to the layer, choose **Layer, Remove Layer Mask**. In the dialog box that appears, click **Apply** to apply the mask to the layer as it is deleted.

How-To Hints

Make Sure That You Paint the Mask

When applying a layer mask, make sure that the mask thumbnail is highlighted in the **Layers** palette before you make any changes. As you're working, it's easy to forget that the mask thumbnail should be selected; if it's not selected, you'll be painting directly into the image.

End

How to Merge and Flatten Layers

In a complex design, it's not hard to accumulate dozens of layers, which can bloat file size and make it hard to find what you're looking for. Whenever possible, you should look for opportunities to merge and flatten layers to keep the design clean and well ordered. *Merging* layers refers to combining some of the layers in a design while keeping other layers separate. *Flattening* the image involves compressing all the layers into one flat background layer.

Begin

1 Open the File

Choose **File, Open** and select the file you want to modify.

2 Launch the Layers Palette

Choose **Window, Show Layers** to open the **Layers** palette and show all existing layers. In this image file, notice that there are two text layers, a layer that contains the image of the walking man, and an adjustment layer (called **Layer 1**). The **Background** layer contains the basic street scene; the **Welcome to Paris** layer contains the shadow for the text.

3 Merge Multiple Layers into One

To merge two layers into one, drag them one above the other in the **Layers** palette and select the layer at the top of the two. Choose **Layer, Merge Down** to combine the selected layer with the layer below it in the list. The name of the lower layer is used when you combine layers with the **Merge Down** command.

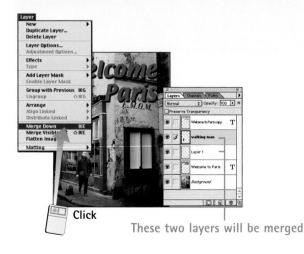

Click

These two layers will be merged

4 Merge the Linked Layers

To merge more than one layer at a time, first link the layers as described in Task 2, earlier in this part. Then choose **Layer, Merge Linked** to combine all the linked layers.

Click

These linked layers will be merged

5 Merge All Visible Layers

An alternative to merging linked layers is to first turn off the visibility of all layers you *do not* want to merge. Choose **Layer, Merge Visible** to combine all visible layers. Then go back to the **Layers** palette and turn the hidden layers back on. The current, or active, layer name is used when you combine layers using the **Merge Visible** command.

Click

These visible layers will be linked

6 Flatten the Image

To reduce all the layers in a document to one, choose **Layer, Flatten Image**. If any layers are hidden as you do this, a dialog box appears, asking whether you want to discard the layer or cancel the operation. Click **Discard** to flatten the image and delete the hidden layers.

Click

All layers are combined

End

How-To Hints

Watch the Layer Order When Merging

If linked layers are not adjacent to each other, the image could be altered when you merge the layers. This is especially true when opacity or blending modes have been used.

Task

PART 12

Building Web Files

*A*dobe has done an excellent job transforming Photoshop from an advanced image-editing tool into an advanced Web-production tool—without losing the image-editing features along the way. With the addition of the ImageReady feature set in Photoshop 5.5, users now can build tables, create JavaScript rollovers, and slice an image into multiple images with custom optimization for each piece.

Note: Much of the work in the tasks in this part will be done in ImageReady and not in Photoshop itself. It is extremely easy to move back and forth between the two programs, calling on the strengths of each as necessary. In fact, the two programs are closely linked, and you can open one from the other and move files back and forth between the applications.

Photoshop and ImageReady automatically optimize, rename, and generate solid HTML code on-the-fly, supporting a wide variety of Web tasks. The code is saved as a separate HTML file that can dovetail with an existing page or, in the case of tables, be used on its own.

Be sure to check out the **HTML** page in the **Preferences** dialog box in both Photoshop and ImageReady to make sure that the code being created is optimized for the platforms and browsers you're developing for. In addition, you should check out the renaming options in the ImageReady **Preferences** dialog boxes to make sure that the autonaming schemes are compatible with your overall process. See Part 1, "Getting Started with Photoshop," for details on setting these preferences. ●

How to Preview Files in Different Browsers and Platforms

Image files look different on Macs than they do on PCs and from browser to browser. PC monitors have a higher gamma than Mac monitors, so images are darker when displayed on PCs. Differences in browser types tend to show themselves when you're building tables or working with other layout issues. When preparing files for the Web, it is imperative that you check each file on all platforms and in as many browsers as possible. This task covers most of your preview options and looks at file-format previews.

Begin

1 Open the File in ImageReady

Because it's easier to preview an image in ImageReady, and because we'll be using some of the features from that program, let's start by opening an image file in ImageReady. To do so, launch the **ImageReady** program and choose **File, Open**. Then select the file you want to preview.

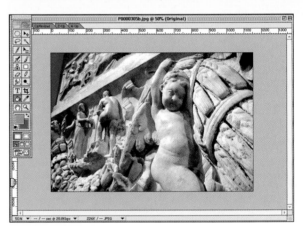

2 Preview for Windows

If you're on a Mac and you want to see what the file will look like on a Windows machine, choose **View, Preview, Standard Windows Color**. This command adjusts the monitor's appearance to reflect the 2.2 Gamma setting typical for most PCs.

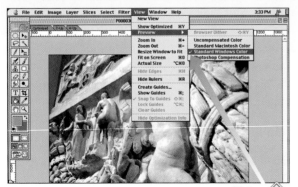

Click

3 Preview for Mac

If you're on a PC and you want to see what the file will look like on a Macintosh, choose **View, Preview, Standard Macintosh Color**. This command adjusts the monitor's appearance to reflect the 1.8 Gamma setting typical for most Macs.

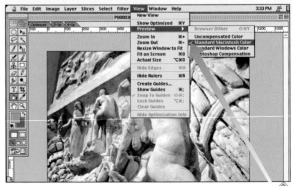

Click

4 Preview as JPEG

After you set the preview to Mac or PC, you should determine the best compression format for your image. To test the results of JPEG compression, choose **Window, Show Optimize** to open the **Optimize** palette. Select **JPEG** from the **Type** drop-down list. Look at the status line at the bottom of the image area: The file's original size appears, followed by the size the file will be if saved as a JPEG. For details on JPEG optimization, see Part 4, Task 7, "How to Build JPEG Files for the Web."

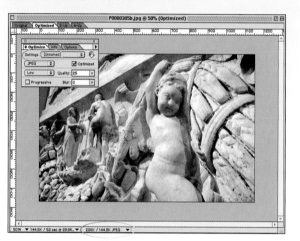

5 Preview as GIF

To test the results of GIF compression, choose **Window, Show Optimize** to open the **Optimize** palette. Select **GIF** from the **Type** drop-down list. Look at the status line at the bottom of the image area: The file's original size appears, followed by the size the file will be if saved as a GIF. For details on GIF optimization, see Part 4, Task 4, "How to Build GIF Files for the Web."

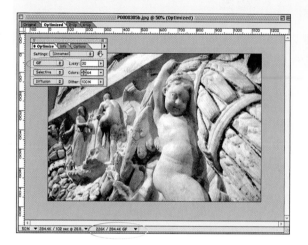

6 Preview in Browsers

To preview a file or table in a browser, choose **File, Preview In, <Browser Name>**. This command launches the specified browser and loads the current file. Here the image is shown in the Netscape Navigator browser.

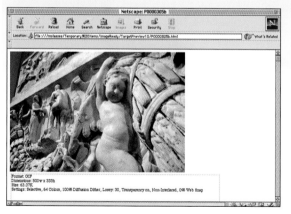

How-To Hints

Set Browser Preferences

To load a browser so that it appears in the **File, Preview In** submenu, you first must create a Windows shortcut or a Mac alias for the browser you want to add to the menu. Then drag the icon for the shortcut or alias into the **Preview In** folder (located in the **Helpers** folder in the **Photoshop** program folder). Restart ImageReady to view the browser in the **Preview In** menu.

End

How to Slice Images for the Web

Slicing an image for the Web involves dividing a larger image into smaller tiles that are assembled in a table as the page is loaded. These smaller tiles often load faster that one large image and are necessary if you want a portion of a large image to act as a *rollover* or an *animation*. ImageReady lets you divide a graphic with a grid of horizontal and vertical lines and then creates individual files on-the-fly—including the necessary HTML code to build the table.

Begin

1 Open the File in ImageReady

From ImageReady, choose **File, Open** and select the image file you want to modify.

2 Show Rulers

If the rulers are not already visible, choose **View, Show Rulers** to display rulers along the top and left sides of the image window.

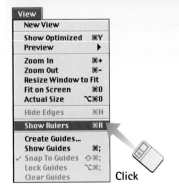

Click

3 Drag Guides

Position the cursor over one of the rulers until it changes to a double-headed arrow. Drag into the image to create a horizontal or vertical guide. Position guides to correspond to the slices you want to create.

Drag

4 Slice Along Guides

Choose **Slices, Create Slices from Guides** to slice the image along the current guidelines. The slices show up on the image area as rectangular sections outlined in blue. The currently selected slice appears in gold.

Click

5 Optimize Slices

Click the **Slice Select** tool from the toolbox and click the first slice in the image area to select it. Then choose **Window, Show Optimize** and set the optimization for that section, just as you would for an entire file. Repeat this step for each slice in the image area. See Part 4, "Converting Files," for more information on using the **Optimize** palette.

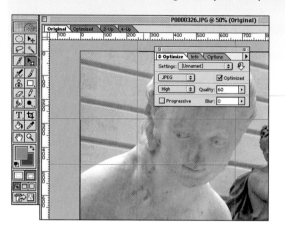

6 Save Files

Choose **File, Save Optimized** to open the **Save Optimized** dialog box. Enable the **Save HTML File** check box if you want ImageReady to create the HTML file for the associated table. If you are saving a large number of slices, you might want to click the **New Folder** button and then name a new folder to keep all the associated files in one place. Click **Save** to save and optimize each slice. Multiple files are created, each file containing a single slice. The files have the original filename and a sequentially assigned number appended to the filename.

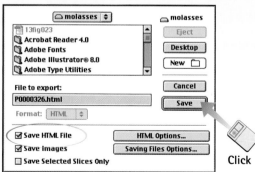

Click

End

How-To Hints

Moving Guides

To reposition a slice guide after you have placed it, click the **Move** tool in the toolbox, position the cursor over the guide, and drag the guide as needed.

Setting Slice Preferences

Use the ImageReady **Preferences** dialog boxes to specify the color and appearance of slices as they are displayed in ImageReady. You can control the tinting, icon size, and especially the naming conventions of the slices as they are created and saved. See Part 1, Task 11, "How to Set ImageReady Preferences," for details.

How to Build Filter-Based GIF Animations

Photoshop and ImageReady enable you to create impressive animation sequences using progressive applications of various texture filters or distortion filters. (You can create the frames in Photoshop as layers, but only ImageReady can create the animation.) By creating duplicate layers of the same file and then applying a filter with increasing intensity, it is easy to animate the filter application. In this task, we take a hazy image of a lake and apply the **Twirl** filter in successive layers to create a nifty animation. Although you can start with any type of file, animations must be saved in the GIF format.

Begin

1 Open the File in ImageReady

In ImageReady, choose **File, Open** and select the file you want to animate with a filter.

2 Duplicate Layers

Choose **Window, Show Layers** to open the **Layers** palette. Choose **Duplicate Layer** from the palette menu multiple times to create several individual states for the animation. In this example, I created three more layers.

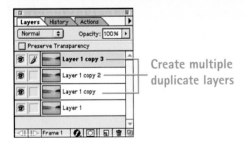

Create multiple duplicate layers

3 Filter the Layers

Select the first layer in the **Layers** palette and open the desired filter (for this example, I chose **Filter, Distort, Twirl**). Apply a modest filter amount and click **OK**. Select the other layers in sequence, applying the filter to each layer with increasing intensity. This figure shows the filter being applied to the last layer. In the **Layers** palette, notice how the thumbnails show the increasing intensity of the **Twirl** filter.

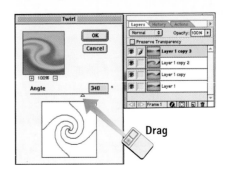

Drag

4 Open the Animation Palette

Choose **Window, Show Animation** to open the **Animation** palette.

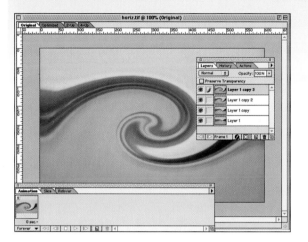

5 Create Frames

Choose **New Frame** from the **Animation** palette menu to create a new animation frame. Repeat this step to create a corresponding frame for each filtered layer you created in Step 3. For example, if you have the original layer and created three filtered copies in Step 3, create four animation frames now.

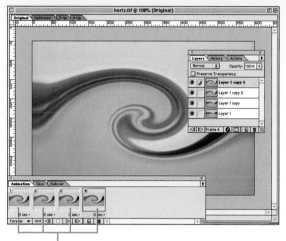

Make as many frames as you have layers

6 Assign Layers to Frames

With both the **Layers** and **Animation** palettes visible, click the first animation frame and select the corresponding first layer of the filter progression. Click the visibility icons (the eye icons) for all the other layers so that only the selected layer is visible. Then click the next animation frame and select the next filtered layer in the **Layers** palette, making sure that only the selected layer is visible. Continue until each frame is assigned to a layer.

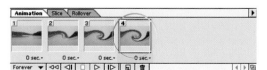

How-To Hints

Begin in Photoshop if Necessary
Because Photoshop offers many more filter options than does ImageReady, you might want to perform Steps 1 through 3 of this task in Photoshop. After you have filtered all the layers, click the **Jump To** button at the bottom of the toolbox to open the file in ImageReady and continue with Step 4.

Continues

7 Play Back in ImageReady

Click the **Play** button at the bottom of the **Animation** palette to play the animation. Check for smoothness, alignment, and timing between frames. The animation will replay continuously; click the **Stop** button to stop the playback.

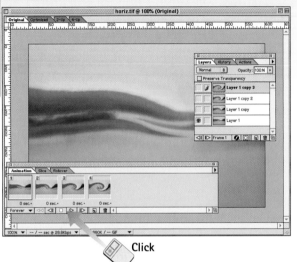

Click

8 Set the Frame Timing

To add a timing delay for a single frame, click the timing pop-up menu at the bottom of the frame and select the desired time delay. For example, you might want to add a longer delay to the first frame to emphasize the original state of the image.

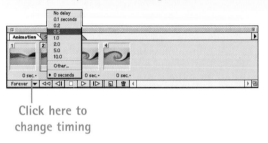

Click here to change timing

9 Set GIF Optimization

Choose **Window, Show Optimize** and optimize the animation as a GIF file. See Part 4, "Converting Files," for details on GIF file optimization.

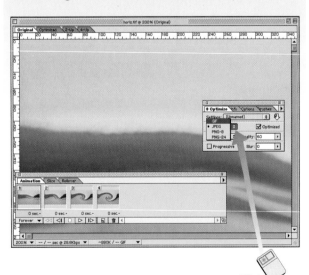

Click

10 Preview in a Browser

Choose **File, Preview In** and select the target browser from the **Preview In** submenu. The animation file opens in the specified browser, with information about the file size, file type, and compression type displayed at the bottom of the window.

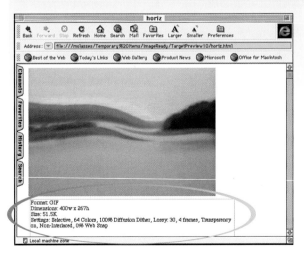

11 Save as GIF

Choose **File, Save As** to open the **Save As** dialog box. Select the GIF file format and rename the file as necessary. Click **Save** to save the animation with the specified settings.

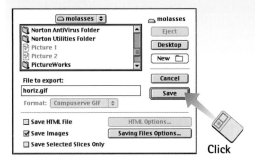

Click

End

How-To Hints

Optimizing and Saving

Although you optimized the image file as a GIF in Step 9 of this task, you must also save the file as a GIF in Step 11. Optimizing the file as a GIF sets the number of colors and so on; it does not save the file. You must save the file using the GIF format, or the file will not animate.

Keep the Number of Animation Frames to as Few as Possible

Animation frames dramatically increase file size—and consequently download times. Keep the number of frames to a minimum to ensure fast download times and to guarantee fast-loading pages.

How to Build Color-Based GIF Animations

Color-based animations are based on images that change and cycle colors without affecting the position of the objects in the image. These color shifts can be fast and dramatic, or they can be subtle and gradual. Because ImageReady has limited color controls, this task begins in Photoshop and switches to ImageReady to build the animation. Consider using **Hue/Saturation**, **Color Balance**, **Curves**, **Replace Color**, and **Selective Color** to make the Photoshop color changes.

Begin

1 Open the File in Photoshop

In Photoshop, choose **File, Open** and select the image file you want to animate with color changes.

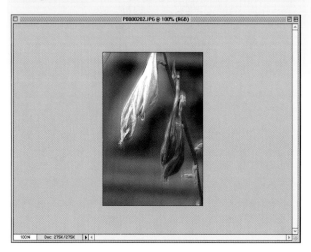

2 Duplicate Layers

Choose **Window, Show Layers** to open the **Layers** palette. Choose **Duplicate Layer** from the palette menu multiple times to create several individual states for the animation. In this example, I duplicated the layer three times.

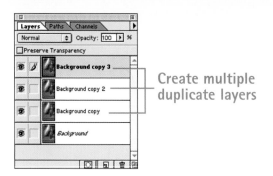

Create multiple duplicate layers

3 Filter the Layers

Select the first layer in the **Layers** palette and open the desired color control (in this example, I chose **Image, Adjust, Hue/Saturation**). Modify the color in the first layer and click **OK**. Select the other layers in sequence, applying the color change to each layer with increasing intensity. Notice that the thumbnails in the **Layers** palette reflect the changes you are making.

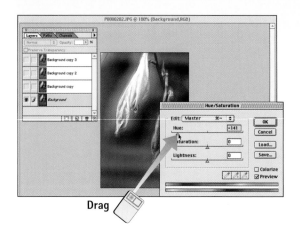

Drag

4 Jump to ImageReady

Click the **Jump To** button at the bottom of the toolbox to open the file in ImageReady. If you're working with a newly created image in Photoshop, you'll be asked to save the file before opening it in ImageReady. Simply save the image as a .PSD file and continue.

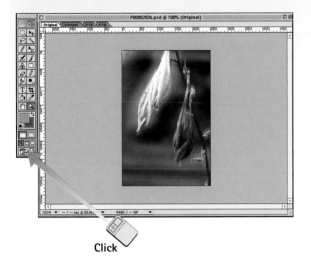

Click

5 Create Frames

Choose **Window, Show Animation** to open the **Animation** palette. Choose **New Frame** from the **Animation** palette menu to create a new animation frame. Repeat this step to create a corresponding frame for each adjusted layer you created in Step 3. For example, if you have the original layer and created three adjusted copies in Step 2, create four animation frames now.

Make as many frames as you have layers

6 Assign Layers to Frames

With both the **Layers** and **Animation** palettes visible, click the first animation frame and select the corresponding first layer of the color progression. Click the visibility icons (the eye icons) for all the other layers so that only the selected layer is visible.

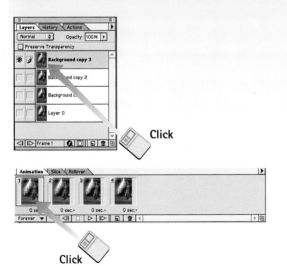

Click

Click

7 Assign the Next Frame

Now click the next animation frame and select the next layer in the **Layers** palette, making sure that only the selected layer is visible. Continue until each frame is assigned to a layer.

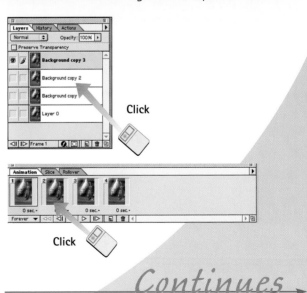

Click

Click

Continues

HOW TO BUILD COLOR-BASED GIF ANIMATIONS **223**

8 Play Back in ImageReady

Click the **Play** button at the bottom of the **Animation** palette to play the animation. Check for smoothness and timing between frames. The animation will replay continuously; click the **Stop** button to stop the playback.

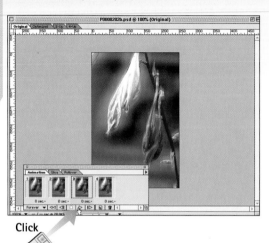

Click

9 Set the Frame Timing

To add a timing delay for a single frame, click the timing pop-up menu at the bottom of the frame and select the desired time delay. For example, you might want to add a longer delay to the first frame to emphasize the original state of the image.

Click here
to chang
timing

10 Set GIF Optimization

Choose **Window, Show Optimize** and optimize the image as a GIF file. See Part 4, "Converting Files," for details on GIF file optimization.

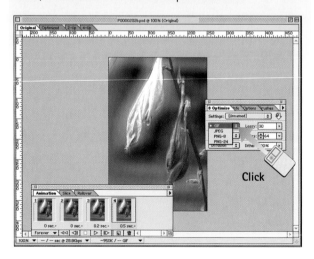

Click

11 Preview in Browser

Choose **File, Preview In** and select a target browser from the **Preview In** submenu. The file opens in the specified browser, with file size, file type, and compression information displayed at the bottom of the window.

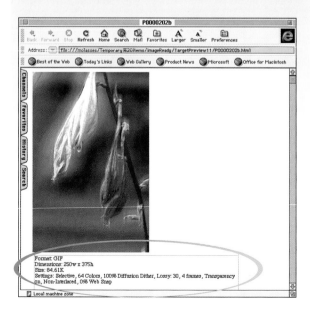

12 Save as GIF

Choose **File, Save As** to open the **Save As** dialog box. Save the file as a GIF file, renaming it if necessary.

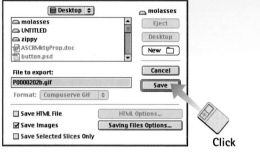

Click

End

How-To Hints

Beware of Preview Speeds

The animation speed might be faster when you are previewing it in the browser than when the file actually is posted online. This may be true because of the bandwidth restrictions of different modems as well as the inherent speed of reading a file locally on your system. In most cases, you should try to keep animation file sizes to 20KB or less. You also should preview the animation online before making the animation publicly available.

How to Build JavaScript Rollovers

Rollover animations are graphics that change as you pass your mouse over a specific spot onscreen. These animations are useful for emphasizing links, especially in graphics that may not be clearly marked. Rollovers consist of a normal state, a mouse-over state, and a click state, so this task creates a separate image variation for each state. To illustrate the rollover effect, this task creates a basic button and then changes the state of the button. After you create the button and its three states, you must save the HTML code as well as the graphics and then paste the code into the target Web page.

Begin

1 Create a New ImageReady File

In ImageReady, choose **File, New** to open the **New Document** dialog box so that you can create a new file. For this task, give the document the filename **button**, specify a height and width of **72** pixels for the image size, and select the **Transparent** radio button. Click **OK**.

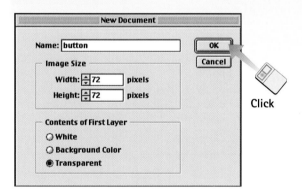

Click

2 Create the Button

Set the foreground color to the color you want to use for the button you'll be drawing. Select the **Ellipse** tool and drag within the image to draw an ellipse the size of the final button. Fill the button shape with the foreground color.

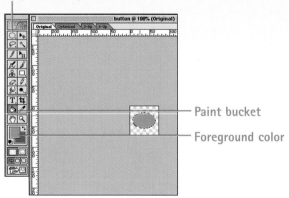

Elliptical marquee

Paint bucket

Foreground color

3 Add the Layer Effect

To give the button a 3D effect, choose **Layer, Effects, Bevel and Emboss**. Set the desired parameters in the **Bevel and Emboss** palette. Deselect the button image to view the effect of the bevel.

4 Make Layer Duplicates

From the **Layers** palette menu, choose **Duplicate Layer** to copy the button and its bevel effect. Choose **Duplicate Layer** again to create a total of three layers, each of which shows the same button and bevel.

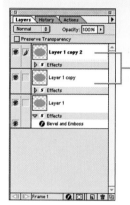

Make two copies of the original image layer

5 Color the Layers

Color the layers for the various button states: original, mouse over, and clicked: In the **Layers** palette, select the first duplicate layer and choose **Image, Adjust, Hue/Saturation**. Drag the **Hue** slider to change the color of the button; click **OK**. In the **Layers** palette, select the second layer. Open the **Hue/Saturation** dialog box, and adjust the **Hue** slider to change the color of the button on this layer to a third color. Click **OK**.

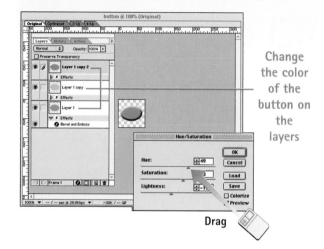

Change the color of the button on the layers

Drag

6 Create Rollover States

Choose **Window, Show Rollover** to open the **Rollover** palette. Select **New State** from the palette menu to create a new state caller **Over**. Select **New State** again to create another new state called **Down**. You now should have a total of three states: **Normal**, **Over**, and **Down**. (And, unbeknownst to you, ImageReady is creating the JavaScript code to make all this work!)

ImageReady creates these for you.

7 Assign Layers to States

In the **Rollover** palette, select the **Normal** state; in the **Layers** palette, select the layer that shows the color you want the button to be in its normal state. In the **Rollover** palette, select the **Over** state and assign to it a different layer from the **Layers** palette. Then select the **Down** state and assign to it the third layer color. Choose **File, Save Optimized** to save the file, making sure that the **Save HTML File** check box is enabled.

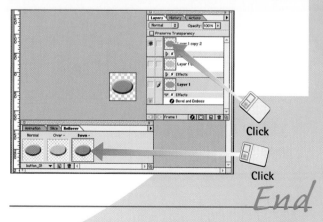

Click

Click

End

How to Build a Web Photo Gallery

The **Web Photo Gallery** feature in Photoshop is a great way to quickly post to the Web a thumbnail directory of images that includes links to full-sized images, filenames, and the photographer's name and date. Anyone who wants to post a directory of images should take advantage of this feature, which is built around Photoshop's **Actions** technology. Users place images into a single folder, set the parameters, and step back. The script runs everything right before your eyes, building the code, optimizing the images and thumbnails, and creating all the links.

Begin

1 Select Web Photo Gallery

In Photoshop, choose **File, Automate, Web Photo Gallery** to open the **Web Photo Gallery** dialog box.

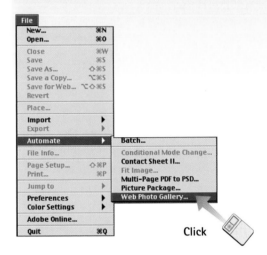

Click

2 Set the File Source and Destination

In the **Files Source** section, click the **Choose** button and navigate to the source folder (the folder that contains all the raw images). Click **Open** or **OK**. In the **Files Destination** section, click the **Choose** button and navigate to the destination folder (where the final files and HTML documents will be stored). Click **Open** or **OK**.

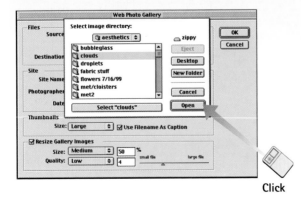

Click

3 Name and Date the Site

In the **Site** section of the dialog box, fill in all appropriate fields, listing the site name, date, and photographer information. In the **Thumbnails** section, select the size of the thumbnails from the **Size** pop-up menu. Enable the check box if you want to use the filenames as captions for the thumbnails.

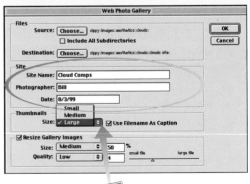

Click

4 Resize Images

Enable the **Resize Gallery Images** check box if you want to resize the main images that open from the thumbnails. With this box enabled, choose the image size from the **Size** pop-up menu and the JPEG compression rate from the **Quality** pop-up menu. To enter a specific JPEG compression value, select the quality setting from the **Quality** slider.

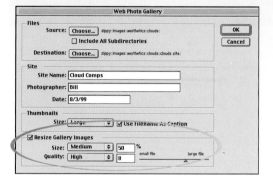

5 Build the Site

Click **OK** to build the Web Photo Gallery site. Photoshop runs the script on its own, opening files, compressing, and saving everything to the source folder you specified in Step 2. Depending on the number and complexity of the files in your source folder, this process can take some time.

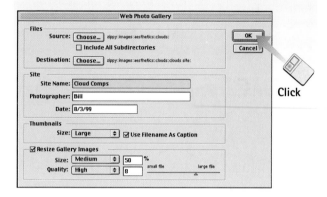

Click

6 Test the Site

When the script is complete, Photoshop launches the Web Gallery in a browser window for you to test. Click the thumbnails to test the links and make sure that everything is listed properly.

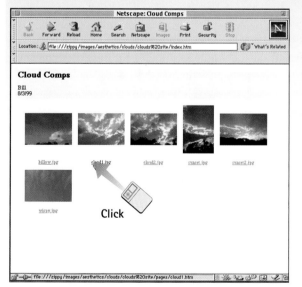

Click

How-To Hints

File Structure

Photoshop creates several files and folders within the source folder you designated to support the Web Photo Gallery. All the images are stored in an **images** folder; thumbnails go into a **thumbnails** folder. A separate HTML page also is created for each image and is stored in a folder called **pages**. The main gallery page is called **index.htm**. When posting your gallery page online, be sure to include all these elements on your server.

End

Task

PART 13

Special Effects

*Y*ou can perform two basic kinds of tasks with Photoshop. One is the basic, utilitarian task of image processing, and the other is the dynamic, eye-catching effect you can create by using filters and special Photoshop commands.

Until this point, you've only looked at the image-processing side of things—exploring how to crop, rotate, and paint images. Although you almost always will need these skills more than you will need creative special effects, the reality is that special effects are just more fun. To that end, the tasks in this part look at a variety of special effects you can apply fairly easily in Photoshop.

A good special effect is often the result of a careful selection so that the effect applies to only a portion of the image. A good special effect might also combine a filter or effect with surrounding layers or the previous image state. By creating effects in combination or by applying them to specific areas, you can create effects that are professional and distinctive.

This part spends a fair amount of time looking at various filter options; with more than 100 native Photoshop filters built into version 5.5, we won't scratch the surface of all that's available. I've selected certain filters you can combine with other effects, such as Blur or Lighting effects. The filters I've selected also let me explain the general approach to working with filters, emphasizing the use of the **Fade** command and the filter color selection.

Of the filters not covered here, be sure to check out the **Artistic** and **Brush Strokes** filters, which create a staggering variety of strokes, textures, and abstractions. ●

How to Build a Glow Effect with Stroke Path

You can add an effect that looks like a glowing halo around a featured object that softly fades into the background. In addition to having aesthetic appeal, the effect described in this task works well when you're silhouetting an object against a white or dark background. It also works to separate the object from its background.

Begin

1 Open the File and Draw a Path

Choose **File, Open** and select the file you want to modify. Select the **Pen** tool from the toolbox. Use the techniques described in Part 3, "Selection Techniques," to draw a path around the desired object.

2 Select the Outside of the Object

Choose **Window, Show Paths** to open the **Paths** palette. With the path selected, choose **Make Selection** from the palette menu and click **OK** in the **Make Selection** dialog box that appears. Then choose **Select, Inverse** to deselect the object and select only the background.

— The background is selected

3 Select the Glow Color

Double-click the **Foreground** color swatch in the toolbox; after the **Color Picker** opens, select a color for the glow. Click **OK** to close the **Color Picker**.

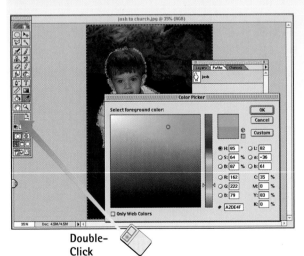

Double-Click

4 Configure Airbrush Settings

Double-click the **Airbrush** tool in the toolbox to open the **Airbrush Options** palette. Drag the **Pressure** slider to about 8 or 10 percent and select a very large feathered brush.

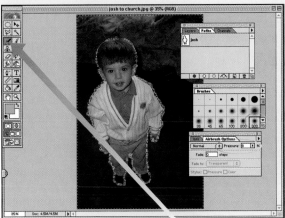

Double-
Click

5 Stroke the Path

With the new path selected in the **Paths** palette, select **Stroke Subpath** from the palette menu. In the **Stroke Path** dialog box that appears, click **OK** to apply the stroke using the airbrush settings specified in Step 4.

6 Modify Airbrush Settings

Restroke the path several times by repeating Steps 4 and 5. Each time you reapply the stroke, select a smaller brush size and increase the pressure. This intensifies the stroke as it gets close to the object, simulating the glow effect. From the **Paths** palette menu, choose **Turn Off Path** to see the image without the selection handles.

How-To Hints

Hide the Path

It can be hard to evaluate the effect of the stroke while the path is selected, because the outline of the path obscures the image edge. After you apply each stroke, you may want to deselect the path in the **Paths** palette. After evaluating the stroke results, reselect the path (by clicking with one of the **Pen** tools) and continue building the effect.

Other Path-Creation Methods

You also can use any of the other techniques described throughout this book to create a selection. For example, you can use Quick Mask to paint your selection, or you can use the Magnetic Lasso tool. After you create the selection, you can easily transform it into a path by clicking the Makes work path from selection icon at the bottom of the Paths palette. You can then edit the path using any of the Pan tools from the Tool palette.

End

How to Create Lighting Effects

The **Lighting Effects** filter casts multiple spotlights of different colors, falling across the image as though it were a flat surface. The filter gives you full control over the focus and direction of the light, as well as the color, exposure, surface texture, and ambient light characteristics. Use this filter to add depth and drama to an image, as well as to build interest into a composition by highlighting a focal point.

Begin

1 Open the File

Choose **File, Open** and select the file you want to modify.

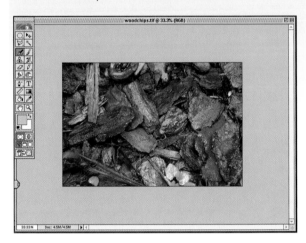

2 Select Lighting Effects

Choose **Filter, Render, Lighting Effects** to open the **Lighting Effects** dialog box. You will see a thumbnail of the image on the left side of the dialog box, with one spotlight already placed over the image.

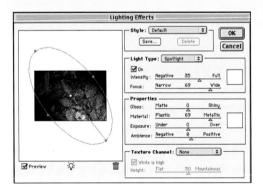

3 Reposition the Light

Click and drag the center of the light to reposition the light circle in relation to the thumbnail image. Then click the point where the light-source line meets the light circle and drag to move the light source. Finally, drag the handles on the light circle to widen or narrow the light beam as it is cast on the image.

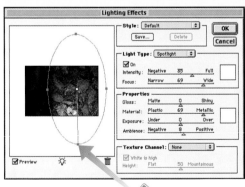

Drag

4 Configure the Light Type

Modify the **Intensity** and **Focus** sliders as desired to brighten the image and focus the light beam. Click the color swatch slider to display the **Color Picker** so that you can select a color for the light itself.

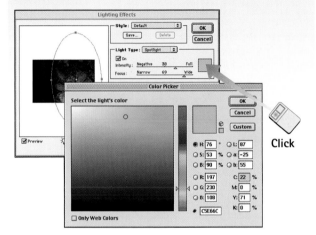

Click

5 Configure Properties

The four **Properties** sliders control the appearance of the surface of the image as well as the overall brightness of the exposure. Adjust the **Gloss** and **Material** sliders to modify the surface brightness. The **Exposure** slider controls image brightness, and the **Ambience** slider controls the amount of secondary ambient light. You can click the color swatch in this area of the dialog box to modify the color of the ambient light.

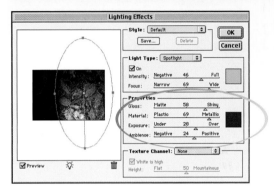

6 Add Other Lights As Needed

To add other light sources, click and drag the light bulb icon into the thumbnail image. Reposition and reset the parameters as described in Steps 3 through 5. The **Style** drop-down list at the top of the **Lighting Effects** dialog box contains many more fun options you can experiment with. If you want to remove a light, you can do so by dragging it to the trash can icon at the bottom of the dialog box. Keep in mind that you need at least one light source.

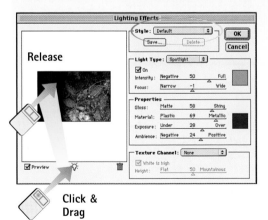

Release

Click & Drag

End

How-To Hints

Other Kinds of Light

In addition to spotlights, you can use omni-directional lights and directional lights. *Omni lights* radiate light equally in all directions from the center point; *directional lights* cast an even blanket of light across the entire image. Select **Directional** and **Omni** lights from the **Light Type** drop-down list in the **Lighting Effects** dialog box.

Using Presets

The **Style** drop-down list in the **Lighting Effects** dialog box offers 16 lighting presets. In addition to exploring these options, you can save your own combinations by clicking the **Save** button and naming the effect in the **Save As** dialog box that appears. This option saves the current configuration of Lighting Effects settings as a preset, which then appears in the **Style** list.

How to Apply a Radial Blur

A *radial blur* is an interesting effect that blurs an image in toward a center point, or rotates it around a center point. The effect is similar to the photography technique of making a zoom lens time exposure that creates a tunnel effect in toward the subject. This is a good way to create emphasis on a central subject or image area, and to control the composition as a whole.

Begin

1 Open the File and Select the Filter

Choose **File, Open** and select the file you want to modify.Choose **Filter, Blur, Radial Blur** to open the **Radial Blur** dialog box.

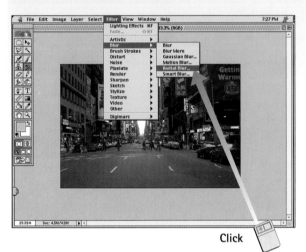

Click

2 Set the Amount Slider

Drag the **Amount** slider to control the degree of blur being applied to the image.

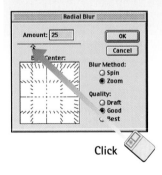

Click

3 Set the Blur Method

Select either **Spin** or **Zoom** to determine whether the blur rotates around a center point in the image or zooms straight into the image.

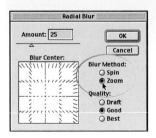

4 Set the Quality Setting

Select **Draft**, **Good**, or **Best** as the **Quality** mode, keeping in mind that the higher the quality, the longer it takes to apply the effect. Note that higher quality does not affect the file size, just the amount of time it takes to display the image.

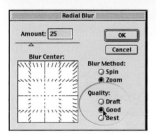

5 Apply the Filter

Click **OK** to apply the **Radial Blur** filter.

End

How-To Hints

Move the Center Point

While working in the **Radial Blur** dialog box, click and drag in the grid preview section to move the center point of the effect. Try to position the center point of the grid over the corresponding focal point of the image.

Fade the Effect

Because the blur effect often obscures much of the image, consider restoring some of the image by choosing **Filter, Fade** immediately after you apply the Radial Blur filter and reducing the opacity or using a blending mode.

How to Add Texture

Texture emphasizes the surface of an image, even as it creates a global graphic effect. Photoshop offers built-in texture maps that simulate sandstone, burlap, canvas, and other surfaces. To apply the Texture filter, you select a surface and then control the light direction and the size of the texture as it is mapped onto the surface of the image.

Begin

1 Open the File and Select the Filter

Choose **File, Open** and select the file you want to modify. Choose **Filter, Texture, Texturizer** to open the **Texturizer** dialog box.

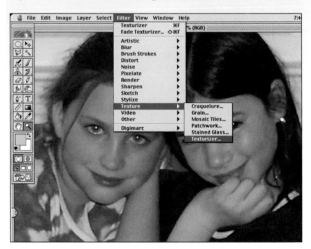

2 Set the Texture Type

From the **Texture** drop-down list box, choose **Brick, Burlap, Canvas,** or **Sandstone**. Notice the results as they appear in the preview window.

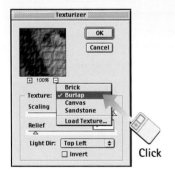

Click

3 Set the Scaling

Scaling refers to the size of the texture effect in relation to the image. In this example, the **Scaling** setting affects how coarse the weave of the burlap looks. Adjust the **Scaling** slider to the desired setting, watching the results in the preview window.

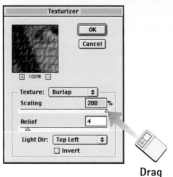

Drag

4 Set the Relief

Relief determines the strength of the texture as it is applied to the image. In this example, the **Relief** setting affects just how "thick" the burlap pattern looks. Adjust the **Relief** slider to achieve the desired effect.

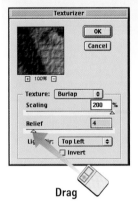

Drag

5 Set the Light Direction

Select a light direction from the **Light Dir** drop-down list. Experiment with selections and observe the effect produced in the preview window.

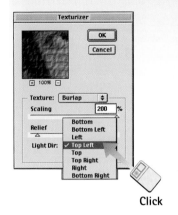

Click

6 Apply the Effect

Click **OK** to close the **Texturizer** dialog box and apply the effect.

End

How-To Hints

Use Other Texture Filters

In addition to the **Texturizer** filter, five other texture filters are offered on the same **Texture** submenu: **Craquelure**, **Grain**, **Mosaic Tiles**, **Patchwork**, and **Stained Glass**. Experiment with all of them to see how they differ and how you can use them to enhance an image.

Click Thumbnail for Before and After Comparison

As you work in the **Texturizer** dialog box, the results of the current settings are displayed in real time in the preview thumbnail. To compare the current state of the image with the original state, click and hold the mouse button while the cursor is over the preview thumbnail; the thumbnail reverts to the original, unaltered image.

How to Add a Lens Flare

Adding a *lens flare* to an image creates a bright spot of light that simulates the lens flare created when a photographer points a camera lens into the sun. Although this is a bad thing for photographers, the lens flare effect often works as a design element, adding a specular accent to a digital composite.

Begin

1 Open the File

Choose **File, Open** and select the file you want to modify.

2 Select the Lens Flare Filter

Choose **Filter, Render, Lens Flare** to open the **Lens Flare** dialog box.

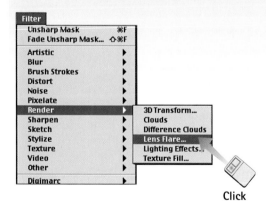

Click

3 Move the Flare Center

A small lens flare preview appears in the **Flare Center** thumbnail of the dialog box. Click and drag the cross at the center of the flare to reposition it in relation to the image.

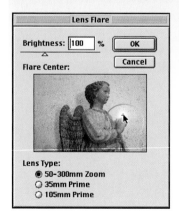

4 Set the Brightness

Adjust the **Brightness** slider to control the intensity of the flare. Observe the effect in the preview window.

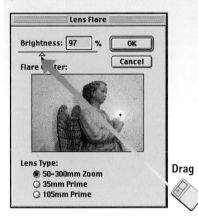

Drag

5 Choose the Lens Type

Select one of the three options at the bottom of the dialog box to specify the type of lens simulated in the effect. Each lens effect mimics the effect of a different focal-length camera lens.

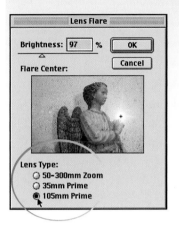

6 Apply the Effect

Click **OK** to close the **Lens Flare** dialog box and apply the filter.

End

How-To Hints

Building Lens Flare Animations

The **Lens Flare** is a perfect filter to use when building a progressive GIF animation, as described in Part 12, Task 3, "How to Build Filter-Based GIF Animations." Increase the brightness progressively in the animation to create the effect of a starburst.

How to Add Noise Texture

In digital imaging, *noise* refers to a coarse, pointillist pattern that is applied to create a graphic feel in an image. Noise is often used when an image is blurry to start with and resists sharpening with Photoshop's standard filters. In this case, you may like the effect when you add noise and create a graphic look for the image, masking the lack of sharpness.

Begin

1 Open the File

Choose **File, Open** and select the file you want to modify.

2 Select the Noise Filter

Choose **Filter, Noise, Add Noise** to open the **Add Noise** dialog box.

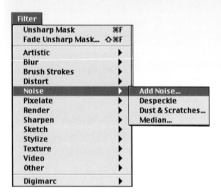

3 Set the Amount

Move the **Amount** slider to control the amount of noise in the image. Observe the effect in both the preview window in the dialog box and in the original image area.

Drag

4 Set the Distribution

Select either the **Uniform** or **Gaussian** option to control how the effect is applied. The **Gaussian** option tends to mimic more closely the noise that appears on the emulsion of photographic film.

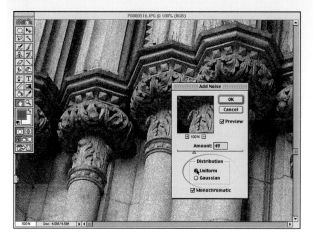

5 Select the Monochromatic Effect

Enable or disable the **Monochromatic** check box and observe the effect this option has on the image. By default, noise is added to an image using randomly colored pixels. These colors can be distracting in some images; the **Monochromatic** option adds noise using grayscale pixels.

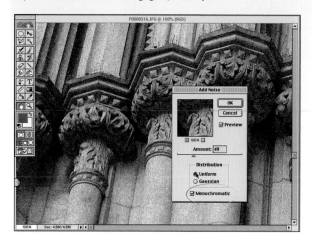

6 Apply the Effect

Click **OK** to close the **Add Noise** dialog box and apply the effect.

End

How-To Hints

Noise on a Layer

Instead of applying the **Noise** filter directly to the image, create a new layer filled with a color. Apply the **Noise** filter to the new layer and then adjust the opacity or blending modes to combine it with the image layer. This approach lets you turn the effect on and off and apply it selectively using layer masks (see Part 11, Task 6, "How to Add a Layer Mask").

How to Simulate Photo Grain

Photoshop enables you to simulate the softer grain effects found in photography. This effect works well when you need to emphasize the photographic aspects of an image, while adding a uniform graphic feel. The only problem with the Photoshop **Grain** filter is that the grain is rendered in a spectrum of bright colors—which is nothing like the grain found in photography. To create more natural colors, this task converts the image to Lab color and isolates the effect to the **Lightness** channel to maintain natural color.

Begin

1 Open the File and Convert to Lab Color

Choose **File, Open** and select the file you want to modify. Choose **Image, Mode, Lab Color** to convert the image into Lab color mode. In this example, we are using Lab color so that we can add a special effect to the **Lightness** channel without affecting the other color channels.

2 Select the Lightness Channel

Choose **Window, Show Channels** to open the **Channels** palette. Highlight the **Lightness** channel to select it and click the visibility icon (the eye) for the **Lab** composite image. This action makes only the **Lightness** channel visible and also previews the full composite image.

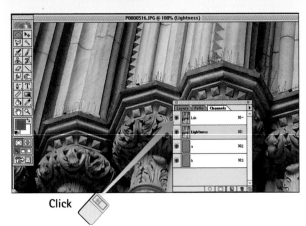

Click

3 Select the Grain Filter

Choose **Filter, Texture, Grain** to open the Grain dialog box.

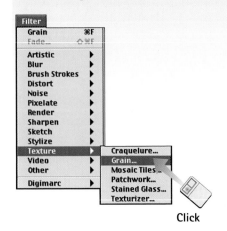

Click

4 Set the Grain Type

Choose the overall grain pattern from the **Grain Type** drop-down list at the bottom of the dialog box. Notice the effect your selection has on the preview window at the top of the dialog box.

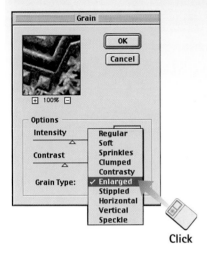

Click

5 Set Intensity and Contrast

Adjust the **Intensity** slider to control the amount of grain applied to the image. Adjust the **Contrast** slider to make the grain pattern more or less pronounced.

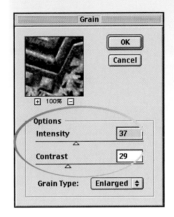

6 Apply the Effect

Click **OK** to close the **Grain** dialog box and apply the effect. Depending on the file format you want to save the file in, you may want to convert the mode back to RGB or CMYK.

End

How-To Hints

Experiment with Grain Type

You can select one of 10 effects from the **Grain Type** list; these effects offer a wide range of styles. Take some time to experiment with the options, choosing the right effect for your image.

How to Posterize an Image

Posterizing an image in Photoshop reduces all areas of an image to flat color, eliminating shading and fine detail. Photoshop allows up to 255 flat colors, so you can work in a fair amount of detail if you choose—but that tends to go against the spirit of the effect, which strives to create the look of a silkscreen poster.

Begin

1 Open the File

Choose **File, Open** and select the file you want to modify.

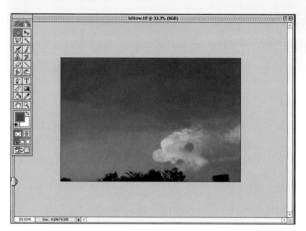

2 Choose Posterize

Choose **Image, Adjust, Posterize** to open the **Posturize** dialog box.

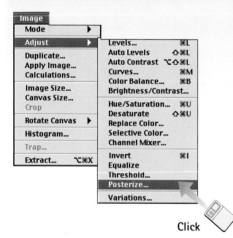

Click

3 Select the Number of Levels

In the **Levels** box, type the number of levels for the effect. This value controls the balance between a smooth and a graphic look in the image by enabling you to set the number of colors, or levels, used for the effect.

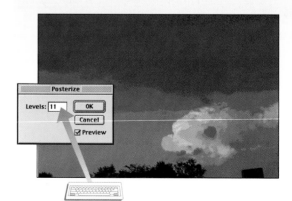

4 Apply the Effect

Click **OK** to close the **Posturize** dialog box and apply the effect.

5 Fade the Effect

Choose **Filter, Fade Posterize** and experiment with the **Opacity** slider and the options in the **Mode** drop-down list box to adjust the posterize effect further. In this example, the **Opacity** is set at **81** percent and the **Overlay** blend mode is used. Click **OK** to close the **Fade** dialog box and apply the effect.

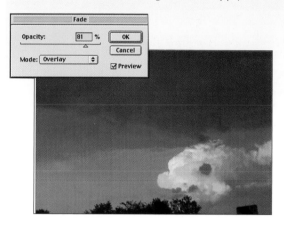

6 Paint Back Details

To add back any detail areas, select the **History Brush** and paint back details from the original image state. Refer to Part 8, Task 4, "How to Use the History Brush," for details.

End

How-To Hints

A Prelude to GIF Images

Use the **Posterize** filter *before* converting an image to a GIF file. This filter helps control colors and color breaks in an image, optimizing the appearance of the image while keeping the number of colors very small.

Color Changes

Photoshop approximates the colors in a posterization based on the resident colors in the image. To change one or more of the colors, choose **Image, Adjust, Replace Colors** and sample and change the colors as needed.

How to Create a Halftone Pattern

The **Halftone Pattern** filter creates a graphic effect that simulates a halftone screen being applied to an image. This effect reduces the image to two colors and creates a stylized graphic feel that is distinctive and unique. The colors used for the filter are taken from the foreground and background colors, so be sure to select these colors before applying the filter, as explained in Step 2.

Begin

1 Open the File

Choose **File, Open** and select the file you want to modify.

2 Select Colors

Because the halftone effect uses the foreground and background colors, you must set these colors before applying the filter. Click the **Foreground** color swatch in the toolbox and choose the desired color from the **Color Picker**. Click the **Background** color swatch and select the second color.

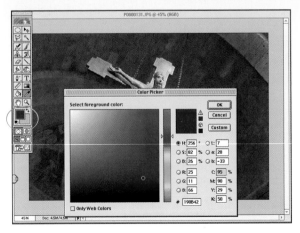

3 Choose the Halftone Pattern Filter

Choose **Filter, Sketch, Halftone Pattern** to open the **Halftone Pattern** dialog box.

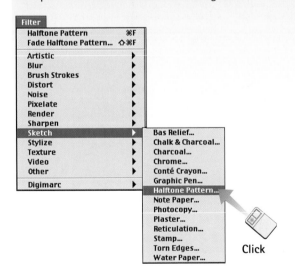

Click

4 Select the Pattern Type

From the **Pattern Type** drop-down list box, choose **Dot**, **Circle**, or **Line** to determine the actual halftone pattern to be used. Observe the effect your selection has on the preview window at the top of the dialog box.

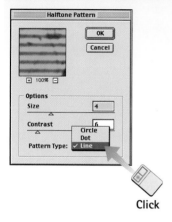

Click

5 Select the Size and Contrast

Adjust the **Size** slider to control the size of the halftone pattern relative to the image. Adjust the **Contrast** slider to control how prominently the effect is applied to the image.

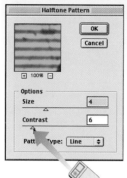

Click

6 Apply the Effect

Click **OK** to close the **Halftone Pattern** dialog box and apply the effect to the image.

End

How-To Hints

Fade with Blending Modes to Combine Effects

Halftone pattern effects work very well with blending modes because of their graphic feel and flat areas of color. When combined with the original image, interesting hybrid effects can be achieved. Choose **Filter, Fade Halftone Pattern** directly after applying the filter to use the blend modes and to change the opacity of the filter.

Switch the Color Order

The **Halftone Pattern** filter applies the foreground color to the shadows and the background color to the highlights. If you don't like the color distribution as initially applied, undo the filter and click the **Switch Colors** icon in the toolbox to reverse foreground and background colors. Reapply the filter and compare the results.

How to Apply a Ripple Effect

Photoshop is full of filter effects that can create wavy, distorted lines within an image. In fact, an entire filter submenu, called **Distort**, is full of these effects. The ripple effect described in this task uses the **ZigZag** filter to create the look of rippling concentric circles across the image surface.

Begin

1 Open the File

Choose **File, Open** and select the file you want to modify.

2 Open the ZigZag Filter

Choose **Filter, Distort, ZigZag** to open the **ZigZag** dialog box.

Click

3 Set the Style

From the **Style** drop-down list, choose a distortion pattern. The pattern you choose is reflected in the wireframe preview window at the bottom of the dialog box and in the preview window at the top of the dialog box.

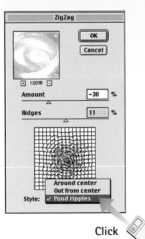

Click

4 Set the Amount

Adjust the **Amount** slider to control the percentage of distortion. Watch the effect of your changes in the preview windows.

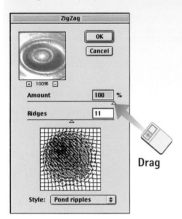

Drag

5 Set the Ridges

Adjust the **Ridges** slider to control how many circular ridges are applied in the pattern.

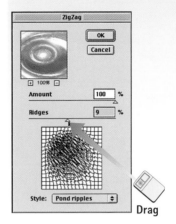

Drag

6 Apply the Filter

Click **OK** to close the **ZigZag** dialog box and apply the filter.

End

How-To Hints

Negative Amounts Implode

Use negative percentages with the **Amount** slider in Step 4 to create an imploding effect that draws into the center rather than emanates out from the center.

How to Brush in a Filter Effect

Instead of applying an effect to an entire image or to a selected area, you can opt to "brush in" an effect using the **History** brush. You have absolute control with respect to the brush size and the opacity of the effect and can create great effects using any of the built-in and plug-in filters available with Photoshop.

Begin

1 Open the File

Choose **File, Open** and select the file you want to modify.

2 Apply a Filter

Apply any of Photoshop's filters to create a desired effect. In this example, we applied the **Conté Crayon** filter to the image.

3 Open the History Palette

Choose **Window, Show History** to open the **History** palette. Click the snapshot at the top of the palette to revert the image to its previous state. The state reflecting the filter application is still in the **History** palette but is grayed out. When you start with the History "snapshot," you have something (an effect) to brush back into the photograph.

Click

4 Set the History Source

Click in the column to the left of the filter state you applied in Step 2 to set the History brush source for the filter effect. In this example, we are setting the History brush so that it will paint in the Conté Crayon filter.

Click

5 Set History Brush Options

Double-click the History brush in the toolbox to open the History Brush Options palette. Set the Opacity as desired and choose a brush size from the Brushes palette.

Double-Click

6 Paint the Effect

Move the cursor into the image and paint with the History brush to selectively brush in the filter effect. In this example, we paint the Conté Crayon filter over the young man's sweater and the background to give it a more textured appearance.

Drag

End

How-To Hints

Apply More Than One Filter

To paint from more than one filter source, apply multiple filters and save a snapshot of each one in the History palette. To save a snapshot, choose New Snapshot from the History palette menu when the filter effect is active. Set the History brush source to the desired snapshot to paint with a specific filter effect.

Glossary

A

actions   Preset scripts that automate repetitive tasks. With just a single mouse click, you can create special effects without having a clue as to how they are done.

adjustment layer   A color-correction layer that allows you to adjust the tone or color in an image without altering the content of the layers beneath it.

alpha channel   The "layer" in which you can save a selection.

anti-aliasing   The method of reducing jagged, pixelated edges in an image or text by slightly blurring the edges of shapes and text to make them appear smooth.

B

baseline shift   Letters that do not sit on the invisible baseline; they "float" above or below it.

bicubic   An interpolation method that delivers the highest quality results when enlarging an image. Other interpolation methods are Bilinear and Nearest Neighbor.

C

canvas   The editable area of a Photoshop file.

clipping paths   A method of exporting a file for use in a vector or layout application. The clipping path format masks out part of the image (for example, you can use this method to drop out the background in a product shot so that only the product object is visible).

CLUT (color lookup table)   *See* GIF file.

CMYK image   A color image that uses the CMYK color model, featuring cyan, magenta, yellow, and black channels.

color model   A way of quantifying color. There are several color models in which you can identify a particular color; CMYK, RGB, HSB, Web, and Lab colors are all supported in Photoshop. In the RGB color model, for example, a specific color is identified as having a particular quantity of red, a particular amount of blue, and a particular amount of green. It doesn't matter which color model you use to identify a color in an image; pick a color model that is compatible with your printing process.

Color Picker   A dialog box from which you can select the foreground or background color. The **Color Picker** displays a window with a range of color in a particular hue; move the **Hue** slider to see a different range of color. Click in the color window to select a color. The selected color is quantified in terms of Hue/Saturation/Brightness, Red/Green/Blue, Lab, CMYK, and hexadecimal (if you need to specify your colors to that degree).

color space   The range of unique colors that can be created for a given color model such as RGB or CMYK.

contact sheet   A Photoshop file that contains thumbnail references for all the images in a given folder. You can use contact sheets to send your client a list of images for approval, to archive, or just to help organize your graphics visually rather than with archaic filenames.

crop   To cut an image down to a specific square or rectangular section, excluding all other unwanted areas.

D

dithering   The process used to fool the human eye into seeing more colors in an image than are really there. The process works by combining two or more existing colors into patterns. When viewed by the human eye, these patterns appear as solid colors.

dot gain   A feature that helps compensate for the ways ink spreads and is absorbed on different kinds of paper. For example, ink spreads a lot more on newsprint than it does on glossy card stock, so you have to compensate to keep the dots from filling in completely.

dots per inch   A term used to determine resolution of a printed image. The number of dots used in a linear inch by a printing or imaging device.

duotone   A grayscale image that is tinted with one color for a graphic effect. Although duotones were originally designed to extend the tonal range of standard grayscale images, designers have embraced them for their graphic look and feel.

E

exposure   The degree of effect applied to the image. You can also think of it as *intensity* or *pressure*.

F

feather   To dissipate the hard-line edge of an area. You can feather a border, for example, so that it "mists" away from the item it surrounds. You can also feather a selection line. When you choose a brush style, you can choose a brush that has a feathered tip.

file extension   The three (or more) letters after the dot in a filename (for example, in `filename.ext`, `.ext` is the extension). The file extension frequently identifies the format of the file. For example, the extension `.txt` tells you that the file is an unformatted text file; the extension `.jpg` tells you the file is a JPEG graphics file.

flatten   In the context of layers, flattening the image involves compressing all the layers into one flat background layer.

G

gamma   A term used to measure relative monitor brightness. Standard gamma settings are **1.8** for Macintosh and **2.2** for Windows.

gamut   The range of unique colors that can be created for a given color model such as RGB or CMYK. Also referred to as *color space*.

GIF file   An efficient, compact file, perfect for use on the Web. GIF files create a color lookup table (CLUT) for each image; each color (up to 256 colors) in the image is categorized and stored in the CLUT. Because of this table (as well as algorithms that track repeating pixels), GIF files compress very well.

gradient   A fill that gradually blends two or more colors together.

grid   An underlying matrix of lines that can be used for general alignment of all items on the page.

guide   A user-defined alignment line that is drawn from the rulers. Guides can also be used in ImageReady to slice an image for use on the Web.

H

halftone   A filter effect that reduces an image to two colors and creates a stylized graphic feel.

histogram   A profile that charts and quantifies the distribution of image pixels across the entire tonal spectrum.

I

image caching   A buffering process that speeds screen redraws and scrolling.

image prep tasks   See pre-processing tasks.

interpolation   The process of enlarging an image file beyond its original scanned attributes. Photoshop interpolation methods are Bicubic, Bilinear, and Nearest Neighbor.

J

JPEG file   A file format that works very well for photographic images because the compression algorithm tends to create artifacts that pixelate the image. Although these effects can degrade the quality of hard-edged graphics, they are easier to hide in photographs.

K

kerning   The spacing between individual pairs of letters.

L

layer mask   A mask that conceals a portion of a layer without actually deleting it, allowing the lower layers to show through those areas of the mask.

layer tile   In the **History** palette, each editing action is represented as a tile. You can click tiles to "peel back" the "layers" of editing changes you have made to an image.

layer   A Photoshop method for separating image components for easy access and editing. Layers follow the metaphor of clear acetate overlays that can be stacked and rearranged.

lens flare   A bright spot of light on an image that simulates the lens flare created when a photographer points a camera lens into the sun.

lossy   A term normally used to describe the nature of the compression method used by the JPEG format. The compression format is referred to as *lossy* because some information is discarded, or lost. It is because of this technique that JPEG images can be compressed to a much smaller file size than images compressed with other formats. In the **Save For Web** dialog box, the **Lossy** option removes colors to create a smaller file size.

M

mask   The process of defining an area of an image or layer for selection, modification, or transparency.

merge   In the context of layers, merging refers to combining some of the layers in a design while keeping other layers separate.

mode Special effects applied from specific toolsets within Photoshop. Modes compare and calculate sets of pixel values, returning results that can be graphic, abstact, or dramatic. Examples of pixel value sets include adjacent layers, brushstrokes over a base image, or filter effects. Therefore, the **Modes** pop-up menu can be found in the **Layers** palette, the **Tools** options palette and the **Filters** menu. When the **Modes** pop-up menu is present, you can select any of the mode options to experiment with the various mode settings. Reset the menu to normal or undo the action to revert to the previous settings.

multiple views More than one window opened for a single image file. You can open two separate windows of the same file, specify a high rate of magnification for editing in one window, and leave the other at full screen size to check your progress as you work.

N

naming format A process that controls the automatic naming of files when new files are created, as used in ImageReady image slicing. When selected from the **File**, **Preferences** menu, names can be automatically generated using a wide range of criteria, such as alphanumeric sequences, date stamping, and file format.

noise A coarse, pointillist pattern that is frequently applied to an already blurry image to create a graphic feel.

O–P

palette One of many control elements you can use to fine-tune your use of Photoshop and ImageReady tools. A palette is associated with a single element of the image (for example, the **Brushes** palette controls the size and shape of the cursor when you are using a painting tool). Each palette has a drop-down menu of options associated with the element it controls.

palette menu When any palette is open, a menu of options specific to that palette is available. Click the right-facing arrow at the top of the palette to display the palette menu of options.

path A linear shape used to define an area within an image. Paths are used to create a selection or mask and can be saved and reloaded without an extreme increase in overall image size..

pixels Dots that serve as the individual building blocks of an image.

plug-in Third-party filters and utilities that extend the basic functionality of Photoshop.

posterize To reduce all areas of an image to flat color, eliminating shading and fine detail.

pre-processing tasks Preliminary tasks that typically clean up an image and get it ready for layout placement or more in-depth editing. These tasks include cropping, rotating, and using the **Unsharp Mask** filter.

Q

quadtone A grayscale image to which are added three colors for a total of four colors (called *plates*).

R

radial blur An interesting effect that blurs an image in toward a center point or rotates it around a center point. The effect is similar to the photographic technique of making a zoom lens time exposure that creates a tunnel effect in toward the subject.

rasterize The process of creating pixel data from vector elements.

relief The strength of a textured filter effect as it is applied to the image. In a Burlap filter, for example, the relief affects the depth of the weave.

render layer To convert a type layer from the scalable, PostScript-based character format to a static, pixel-based format. The conversion is often necessary before other Photoshop effects can be applied.

resolution A term referencing the amount of detail present in a bitmap image, as determined by the number of pixels used. Resolution is determined by multiplying th dots per inch by the overall dimensions, yielding a width and height pixel value.

rollover A graphic that changes as you pass your mouse over a specific spot on the screen.

S

sample point The value of the pixel that sets the color the Background Eraser tool erases. You specify the pixel value by clicking the "sample" the color you want to erase.

scaling The size of a textured filter effect in relation to the image. In a burlap filter, for example, the scaling affects the coarseness of the weave.

scratch disk A Photoshop term referring to the system hard drive that is used as a buffer for storing interim versions of images.

sharpening A method that brings out additional detail in virtually all images except those created on the highest quality scanners. To sharpen an image in Photoshop, you use the **Unsharp Mask** filter.

slice To divide a large image intended for the Web into smaller tiles that are assembled in a table as the page is loaded. These smaller tiles often load faster that one large image and are necessary if you want a portion of a large image to act as a rollover or an animation.

stroke To draw an outline around a selected path. Stroking a path is useful for outlining a rectangle you want to use as a text box, for building buttons for the Web, or for outlining letterforms you may have saved as paths.

T

thumbnail A small graphic that represents a larger image. Thumbnails are often used in palettes to give a visual history of the states in the image.

tonality The grayscale values from 0 to 255 that differentiate an image's pixels. Tonality is black and white and shades of gray; tonality is one of the most expressive elements in an image. If you want to create a strong feeling in an image, consider exaggerating the tonality in some way.

tracking The spacing between entire lines of letters.

transparency checkerboard grid The checkerboard background that appears "through" an image when you have made some part of an image transparent. You can control the size and color of the checkerboard grid using the **Preferences** dialog box.

tritone A grayscale image to which are added two colors for a total of three colors (or plates).

U-Z

vertical type Text arranged in a descending vertical column down the image.

Index

J – K

L

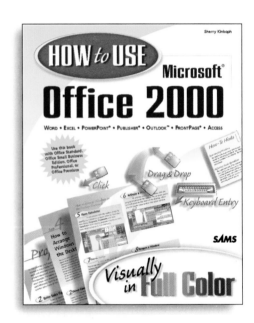